The Nuremberg Trials

Other titles in the World History Series

The Nuremberg Trials

John Davenport

LUCENT BOOKS

An imprint of Thomson Gale, a part of The Thomson Corporation

THOMSON
★
GALE™

Detroit • New York • San Francisco • San Diego • New Haven, Conn. • Waterville, Maine • London • Munich

LIBRARY OF CONGRESS CATALOGING-IN-PUBLICATION DATA

Davenport, John, 1960–
    The Nuremberg trials / by John Davenport.
      p. cm. — (World history)
    Includes bibliographical references and index.
    ISBN 1-59018-634-6 (hard cover : alk. paper) 1. Nuremberg Trial of Major German War Criminals, Nuremberg, Germany, 1945–1946—Juvenile literature. I. Title. II. Series: World history series.
     KZ1176.5.D38 2006
     341.6'9'0268—dc22

                                                2005019446

Contents

Foreword

Each year, on the first day of school, nearly every history teacher faces the task of explaining why his or her students should study history. Many reasons have been given. One is that lessons exist in the past from which contemporary society can benefit and learn. Another is that exploration of the past allows us to see the origins of our customs, ideas, and institutions. Concepts such as democracy, ethnic conflict, or even things as trivial as fashion or mores, have historical roots.

Reasons such as these impress few students, however. If anything, these explanations seem remote and dull to young minds. Yet history is anything but dull. And therein lies what is perhaps the most compelling reason for studying history: History is filled with great stories. The classic themes of literature and drama—love and sacrifice, hatred and revenge, injustice and betrayal, adversity and overcoming adversity—fill the pages of history books, feeding the imagination as well as any of the great works of fiction do.

The story of the Children's Crusade, for example, is one of the most tragic in history. In 1212 Crusader fever hit Europe. A call went out from the pope that all good Christians should journey to Jerusalem to drive out the hated Muslims and return the city to Christian control. Heeding the call, thousands of children made the jour-

ney. Parents bravely allowed many children to go, and entire communities were inspired by the faith of these small Crusaders. Unfortunately, many boarded ships captained by slave traders, who enthusiastically sold the children into slavery as soon as they arrived at their destination. Thousands died from disease, exposure, and starvation on the long march across Europe to the Mediterranean Sea. Others perished at sea.

Another story, from a modern and more familiar place, offers a soul-wrenching view of personal humiliation but also the ability to rise above it. Hatsuye Egami was one of 110,000 Japanese Americans sent to internment camps during World War II. "Since yesterday we Japanese have ceased to be human beings," he wrote in his diary. "We are numbers. We are no longer Egamis, but the number 23324. A tag with that number is on every trunk, suitcase and bag. Tags, also, on our breasts." Despite such dehumanizing treatment, most internees worked hard to control their bitterness. They created workable communities inside the camps and demonstrated again and again their loyalty as Americans.

These are but two of the many stories from history that can be found in the pages of the Lucent Books World History series. All World History titles rely on sound research and verifiable evidence, and all give students a clear sense of time, place, and chronology through maps and timelines as well as text.

All titles include a wide range of authoritative perspectives that demonstrate the complexity of historical interpretation and sharpen the reader's critical thinking skills. Formally documented quotations and annotated bibliographies enable students to locate and evaluate sources, often instantaneously via the Internet, and serve as valuable tools for further research and debate.

Finally, Lucent's World History titles present rousing good stories, featuring vivid primary source quotations drawn from unique, sometimes obscure sources such as diaries, public records, and contemporary chronicles. In this way, the voices of participants and witnesses as well as important biographers and historians bring the study of history to life. As we are caught up in the lives of others, we are reminded that we too are characters in the ongoing human saga, and we are better prepared for our own roles.

Important Dates at the Time

1933
Adolf Hitler is appointed chancellor of Germany.

1936
African American runner Jesse Owens wins four Olympic gold medals in Berlin.

1941
The Japanese attack Pearl Harbor.

1930	1934	1938	1942

1934
Mao Zedong begins the "Long March," a 6,000-mile (10,000km) trek through China to escape opposition forces.

1938
Howard Hughes flies around the world in 3 days, 19 hours, 17 minutes.

1939
World War II begins in Europe with Germany's invasion of Poland.

1942
President Franklin Roosevelt orders the internment of thousands of Japanese Americans.

of the Nuremberg Trials

1943
The artificial kidney is used for the first time on a human patient.

1945
World War II ends in Europe and the Nuremberg Trials begin.

1948
Renowned Indian social reformer Mahatma Gandhi is assassinated.

1953
Sir Edmund Hillary and Tenzing Norgay mount the world's first successful climb to the top of Mount Everest.

1943	1946	1949	1950	1962

1944
Laurence Olivier stars in *Henry V*, considered one of the finest Shakespeare films ever.

1946
Convicted Nazi war criminals are hanged at Nuremberg.

1947
Norwegian explorer Thor Heyerdahl sails the balsa raft *Kon-Tiki* from Peru to Polynesia, proving his theory of ancient migration.

1962
Israel executes Adolf Eichmann for crimes against the Jews and crimes against humanity.

1949
Josef Mengele, the Nazi doctor who sent hundreds of thousands of Jews to their deaths, escapes to South America.

The Crime and the Criminals

It was the worst crime in human history—the ruthless killing of 6 million Jews and the imprisonment, torture, and execution of millions of non-Jews. During World War II (1939–1945) a dark and murderous shadow fell over Europe. It originated in Germany and was called Nazism. Beginning as a radical nationalist political movement, Nazism evolved into a form of government that will forever be associated with cruelty, oppression, and the German attempt to exterminate Europe's Jews.

The veil of hate that descended after the Nazi invasion of Poland in 1939 was not lifted until 1945. In that year the United States, Great Britain, France, and the Soviet Union (Russia) finally defeated the German armies, bringing the war to its conclusion. The utter collapse of Germany ended the nightmare of Nazi rule, but no sooner had that happened than a new drama began. This one involved the process of meting out justice to the men who had ter-

rorized an entire continent in the name of Adolf Hitler and his Nazi Party.

The Nazi Death Machine

For twelve years, from 1933 to 1945, the National Socialist German Workers Party—NSDAP or Nazi Party for short—ruled Germany and dominated the lives of its over 65 million inhabitants. Under the leadership of Adolf Hitler, the Nazis set out to bring a new order to Europe, a new system of values and beliefs based on Nazi ideals. While creating this new order, the Nazis intended to imprison or kill anyone who opposed them politically or failed to measure up to their racial standards.

The people falling into these broad categories included political rivals such as Communists and Socialists, religious minorities, the Sinti and Roma peoples

Adolf Hitler salutes German troops as they march by in review.

(otherwise known as Gypsies), and homosexuals. These people were mercilessly persecuted and quickly found themselves thrown into special prisons known as concentration camps that sprang up throughout Germany in the 1930s. Disabled children and adults, considered a biological threat to German health, were simply murdered. In 1939 Hitler ordered that these unfortunate people constituted "life unworthy of life." It was right, therefore, he said, "that the worthless lives of such creatures should be ended."[1] Operation T-4 was soon begun, a program designed to kill disabled people by means of either lethal injection or poison gas. The most vulnerable Germans felt the Nazi terror first.

Jews and other victims of Nazi atrocities were buried in mass graves like this one located near the Ukranian city of Lvov.

Yet even though many people suffered under the Nazis, only one group was singled out for total global extermination—the Jews. The Nazis viewed the Jews as a racial disease, parasites and bacteria to be cleansed away. Heinrich Himmler, head of the SS (Hitler's security service), spoke of a Germany without Jews as being "deloused": "We are almost deloused," he proclaimed in 1943. "We have only some 20,000 lice left and then it will be ended in all of Germany."[2] Hitler and his followers, drawing on flawed interpretations of Darwin's theory of evolution, saw the Jews as racial and biological enemies who posed a historical and present danger to what the Nazis imagined to be the pure German race. For this reason alone the Nazis decided to annihilate every Jew in Europe. In the end the Nazis succeeded in murdering 6 million of the 11 million in Europe at the time through starvation, labor, torture, shooting, and gassing. Add to this number 3 million Russian and hundreds of American and British prisoners of war, as well as countless other victims, and one has a reign of terror unlike anything ever seen before.

Criminals and Bystanders

Between 100,000 and 250,000 Germans directly took part in some aspect of the killings and persecution. Many millions more helped conquer and administer large areas of Europe for Hitler. The parties involved included the military, government bureaucracy, and most notoriously the SS: The SS (Schutzstaffel) began as Hitler's personal bodyguard in the 1920s but evolved over time into the primary weapon in the Nazi arsenal. Totaling well over a million members, the SS was charged with overseeing the Nazi racial program. It ran the concentration camps and fought alongside the German army as an elite corps known as the Waffen-SS. The SS organized and conducted the mass shootings of Jews in Russia and operated the death camps where Jews were systematically gassed to death from 1942 to 1944.

The men and women who had an active role in what the Nazis called the "Final Solution to the Jewish question" were assisted in their grim tasks by even greater numbers of Germans and non-Germans who stood by and did nothing to stop Hitler. These people either chose to ignore what was happening or lacked the courage to resist. Some were willing to tolerate the torture and murder of others in order to gain advantages for themselves. Most bystanders, however, just did not seem to care enough to stop the Nazis.

Paying the Price

By the end of World War II nearly every German bore some share of the responsibility for what the Nazis had done, and none more so than the Nazi leaders who had dragged Germany into the pit of mass murder and war. Hitler's assistants, those officials who operated the Nazi death machine, were the most responsible. The victors in the war, therefore, sought these men out above all others for arrest and punishment.

Despite great effort, though, many guilty Nazis escaped Allied capture in the spring of 1945. Hitler and his closest aides took their own lives; other top officials slipped out of Europe undetected. Twenty-two of the worst offenders, however, were

The Nazis cremated the bodies of many of the victims in huge ovens like these.

not so fortunate. They were arrested, jailed, and handed over for trial before the International Military Tribunal, a special multinational court established by the Allies for the sole purpose of trying Nazi criminals. The IMT, as it was often called, had no precedent in history. Nations had never pooled their resources in the quest for global justice. Crimes, even large-scale organized ones, had been previously considered a national matter, a concern for those affected but not for other people. Individual countries thus had the job of punishing the criminals. The notion that terror, destruction, and killing during a war might constitute criminal offenses was also new. Brutality had been traditionally viewed as part of the price paid for engaging in armed conflict. Now, for the first time, a court made up of representatives from different countries set itself to the task of prosecuting and punishing wartime atrocities that concerned the entire world.

The Nazis, while fighting a war of aggression, had committed offenses not just in one country but across a whole continent. The IMT, therefore, had the responsibility for guaranteeing the future rule of law everywhere. Between August 1945 and September 1946 lawyers and judges from the United States, Great Britain, France, and the Soviet Union gathered at Nuremberg to confront in court the men who had made the fantasy of a national program of murder a chilling reality.

Chapter One

Taking Prisoners

Nazi Germany lay in ruins in the spring of 1945. Its cities were shattered, its farms and factories destroyed, and the spirit of its people broken. The German nation was about to lose World War II. The Western Allies (the United States, Great Britain, Canada, and France) had defeated the German armies along a line extending from Italy to the Netherlands. The Russians had smashed the Nazi forces in the East. From two sides the Allies had pushed the Germans back into their homeland. One by one, huge chunks of German territory were claimed by the advancing American, British, and Russian divisions. As the nation collapsed, the men who had started the war and murdered millions of innocent people tried to escape. The Nazi leader Adolf Hitler, his propaganda minister Joseph Goebbels, and his SS chief Heinrich Himmler all committed suicide. Other top Nazis went into hiding or fled to South America.

One way or another, as the Second World War in Europe came to an end on May 8, 1945, many Nazis eluded the justice that was due them. Still, not everyone responsible for or involved in Hitler's reign of terror escaped. The Allies, after their military victory, cast a wide net in search of criminals. Over the course of the next year they apprehended hundreds of ex-Nazis. Among the most important were those men who would stand trial at Nuremberg. They included officials who either made possible the Nazi seizure of power or helped Hitler put into action his plan for war and murder. This select group of criminals began to be rounded up before the ink on the surrender documents had dried. Some had to be hunted down; others turned themselves in. Whatever the

Hermann Göring, shown here shortly after his surrender to American troops, signed the order for the systematic killing of European Jews.

The Great Escapees:
Adolf Hitler

The first Nazi to choose death over capture was the once all-powerful German leader or führer, Adolf Hitler. Hitler had been the driving force behind the Nazi project. The entire program had been based on and guided by his ideas and words. Hiding in a concrete bunker beneath the streets of Berlin, according to the postwar testimony of his young secretary and other close associates with him in his underground command post, Hitler listened as Russian tanks moved through the streets above him. He shuddered at the thought of being put on display in a courtroom like some common criminal. In his last testament, detailed in Ian Kershaw's book *Hitler: 1936–1945, Nemesis*, Hitler exclaimed "I do not wish to fall into the hands of enemies who will need a spectacle arranged by Jews."

Determined not to be taken alive, Hitler walked into a small room in his bunker at 3:30 P.M. on April 30, 1945. He sat down next to Eva Braun, the woman he had married just the day before, and each swallowed a poison pill. Hitler, taking no chances that the poison would not work, put a pistol to his head and pulled the trigger. The one man responsible for more suffering and death than humanity had ever known would never stand trial.

Two Russian soldiers point out Hitler's alleged grave. Nearby are the cans of gasoline used to burn the body immediately after his suicide

case, all of the Nazi bosses captured by the Allies stood accused of crimes against the entire world. Many people believed that Nazi leaders should be shot on sight. They felt the same way British prime minister Winston Churchill did when he said that every captured Nazi leader should be "shot to death . . . without reference to higher authority."[3] Churchill saw no need for trials or courts; anyone who had helped Hitler, the prime minister argued, should be immediately executed. The American president, Franklin D. Roosevelt, agreed; the Nazi leadership had to be eliminated without delay. The Russians, however, were firmly behind the idea of public trials. Representatives of the Russian leader Joseph Stalin demanded that there "must be no executions without trial . . . if there were no trials there must be no death sentences."[4] America and Britain eventually agreed with Russia to try the men. The result was that Hitler's most important servants were gathered up and sent to Nuremberg for trial. The architects of the Nazi regime escaped in the end, but the workmen who carried out the regime's policies had to answer for their crimes.

The First Batch Comes In: Göring and Speer

Rudolf Hess, Hitler's deputy leader, had been captured by the British in 1941 after flying to Scotland in an effort to make peace between Great Britain and Germany. He was the first top Nazi to be jailed. Hess, however, was only the first of Hitler's men taken into custody. Throughout late spring of 1945, one Nazi after another was arrested and sent to the detention facilities set up by the Allies. Among the first was Hermann Göring, the nearly three-hundred-pound former chief of Hitler's air force and the führer's second in command. Next in line behind Hitler in the Nazi hierarchy, Göring once proudly exclaimed, "I have no conscience! Adolf Hitler is my conscience!"[5] A confirmed drug addict, Göring boasted that he "was the only man in Germany besides Hitler who had his *own*, underived authority."[6] Göring had a power, in other words, that no one could take away. He demonstrated the extent of that power in July 1941, when at Hitler's command Göring signed the order for the systematic annihilation of Europe's Jews.

Göring, knowing that his high public profile guaranteed capture, gave himself up to the American army on May 9, 1945, just one day after Germany surrendered. As conceited as he was hate filled, Göring brought along suitcases full of clothes, money, jewels, and drugs. Göring loved luxury and saw no reason why a man as important as he should live without the good things in life, even in jail. Göring was used to getting his way; he even tried to bully his captors. When the American general who took him into custody told Göring to give up the baton that identified him as chief of the *Luftwaffe* (air force), he refused. According to witnesses, Göring said, "General, I can't give this to you. It is a symbol of my authority." Infuriated, the American officer bellowed, "You have no more authority. Hand it over!"[7]

Göring was held in an American-run jail when the next big-name Nazi, Albert Speer, was arrested. Intelligent, precise, and emotionless, Speer had worked first as Hitler's personal architect, the man in charge of coordinating Nazi building projects. He later served as the Nazi armaments minister. In that job Speer had been responsible for building the tanks, planes, and guns that made up the Nazi war machine. He was determined to meet every deadline and quota for weapons, even if it meant using and abusing slave laborers. These workers' lives meant little to Speer, except in terms of reaching the production goals the government set. Under Speer's direction, thousands of prisoners, Jews and non-Jews, died in German armament plants.

On May 23, 1945, British troops arrested Speer at his home. When questioned about his activities, Speer presented himself as nothing more than a hardworking technician, a bureaucrat who had nothing to do with any crimes. During the war, however, according to his friend Adolf Galland, an air force general, Speer knew all about the murder of the Jews. "Everybody knew about the concentration camps. Speer, too, of course," Galland reported. "After all, that was where many of his foreign workers were kept."[8] Heinrich Himmler once openly told Speer that the SS was murdering every Jew it could find. Himmler later said in a 1944 speech to SS commanders that Speer was a close partner of his.

Speer, despite knowing clearly what Hitler and Himmler were up to, remained calm and businesslike as he was led off by his captors. In the months to come, Speer would continue to act like a man who simply got caught up in events that were far larger than he. It was all part of a clever strategy of denial.

Governor Frank and the Generals

Speer attempted in the coming months to portray himself as having only the weakest connections to Hitler and his policies. Hans Frank, the next Nazi to be captured, could not defend himself the way Speer did. He had taken a clear and up-front role in the worst Nazi crimes. As the German governor of Poland, Frank had helped organize the cold-blooded murder of nearly 3 million Jews. He also had sent eight hundred thousand forced workers to Germany. Poland, which Frank ruled like a king, was the location of the infamous death camps of Chelmno, Majdanek, Belzec, Sobibor, Treblinka, and Auschwitz. It was here that Frank followed through on the promise he made in 1941: "We must annihilate the Jews wherever we find them. . . . [Poland] will have to become free of Jews."[9]

Frank was captured in late May 1945 disguised as a regular German soldier. His captors discovered his real identity only after Frank drew attention to himself by trying unsuccessfully to commit suicide. He was immediately given over to the officials in charge of jailing leading Nazis.

Other early captures included the military chiefs of Hitler's Germany. American and British forces had arrested General Wilhelm Keitel, General Alfred Jodl, and Admiral Karl Dönitz, all by the end of May. Keitel, chief of the OKW (*Oberkommando der Wehrmacht*), Hitler's central military command, had been so loyal to the führer that behind his back people called him "Lakeitel," or lackey. A lackey is someone who is so weak that they will do any-

Albert Speer (in white trench coat), shown here with General Alfred Jodl and Admiral Karl Dönitz, denied all knowledge of Nazi atrocities.

thing to make those in power happy. When Hitler wanted the army to assist the SS killing squads in Russia, for example, Keitel wrote orders telling his soldiers to do so. He justified himself at the time by saying that Jews were always and everywhere enemies of the German people; they had no right to be given any sympathy whatsoever. Keitel never lost faith in his führer. "Even today," Keitel said from his jail cell in the summer of 1945, "I am a convinced [follower] of Adolf Hitler."[10]

Jodl, Keitel's chief of staff, also thought Hitler was a genius. He praised Hitler as the one man "destined by fate to lead [Germany] to a brighter future."[11] A brighter future for Jodl meant one without Jews. The general hated them and once said that it was unthinkable to live in a world where Jews were considered to be anything other than subhuman slaves. Keitel's chief of operations was devoted to Hitler and the Nazi cause. Jodl did everything he could to help Hitler realize his dream of winning the war and creating a Jew-free world.

The Great Escapees: Joseph Goebbels

No sooner had Hitler committed suicide than one of his most loyal servants, Joseph Goebbels, followed suit. Goebbels had been the führer's propaganda minister. He served as Hitler's voice to the German people for twelve years and was a true believer in the Nazi cause. Sticking by Hitler's side in his bunker until the very end, Goebbels and his wife also preferred death to capture. They saw nothing worth living for without Hitler. "The world that will come after the Führer and national socialism won't be worth living in," Magda Goebbels wrote in a letter recorded by her husband's biographer Ralf Georg Reuth in *Goebbels*. The day after Hitler killed himself, Magda Goebbels poisoned her six children, and Goebbels and she then popped cyanide capsules in their mouths and died.

German propaganda minister Joseph Goebbels and his wife (shown here with three of their children) committed suicide as Allied forces closed in on Berlin.

Karl Dönitz, head of the German submarine service and the navy's top admiral after 1943, had been so close to Hitler that the führer, in his will, asked Dönitz to replace him as leader of Germany. After Hitler's death Dönitz took charge of a defeated Nazi government for twenty-three days before surrendering to British troops in northern Germany. An ardent Nazi supporter throughout the war, Dönitz had once ordered the survivors of attacks by his submarines to be abandoned at sea. He had also turned a blind eye to the fact that submarine crews wore felt boot insulators made from the hair of murdered Jewish women. Dönitz joined his companions in jail, no longer an admiral but a war criminal.

The Arrests Continue

May was a successful month for American and British authorities who worked to capture the perpetrators of Nazi crimes. Hess, Göring, Speer, Frank, and the military leadership represented the top rungs of the Nazi ladder. With each passing day in late May and early June 1945 Allied forces took even more of Hitler's underlings into custody. One by one the men who ran the German government, organized labor for Speer's factories, broadcast Nazi lies at home and abroad, and operated Hitler's security services were arrested.

The Russians, who occupied eastern Germany, captured Grand Admiral Erich Raeder, the chief of the German navy until 1943. They also took into custody Joseph Goebbels' assistant at the propaganda ministry, Hans Fritsche. The French netted Konstantin von Neurath, Hitler's first foreign minister. Julius Streicher, the vicious Jew-hater and publisher of the Nazi newspaper *Der Stürmer*, was disguised as a simple villager when he was arrested by American soldiers. One of the soldiers remembered how his patrol drove up to the house where Streicher was hiding and had this exchange with him: "'What do you think of the Nazis?' the officer in charge said. Streicher responded, 'I am an artist and have never bothered about politics.' 'But you look like Julius Streicher,' the American replied. 'How did you recognize me?' Streicher shouted."[12] With that, perhaps the most vocal and crudest Nazi propagandist went to jail.

By midsummer of 1945 the list of imprisoned Nazis had grown long indeed. Former vice-chancellor Franz von Papen, who had engineered Hitler's seizure of power in 1933, was taken into custody. Ernst Kaltenbrunner, head of the SD (*Sicherheitsdienst*, or security service), responsible for sending people to concentration camps or killing people who opposed Hitler, was picked up by the Americans in the Austrian Alps. Kaltenbrunner's partner in the government, Interior Minister Wilhelm Frick, was apprehended soon after. Fritz Sauckel, the man who organized slave labor for Speer's factories, was hiding in a cave when he decided to turn himself in. Robert Ley, head of the Reich Labor Front, another source of workers for German industry, was discovered by American troops in a Bavarian cabin, dressed in a pair of pajamas. At first he denied being one of Hitler's men; he said his name was Dr. Ernst Distelmeyer. While being questioned, however, an old acquaintance

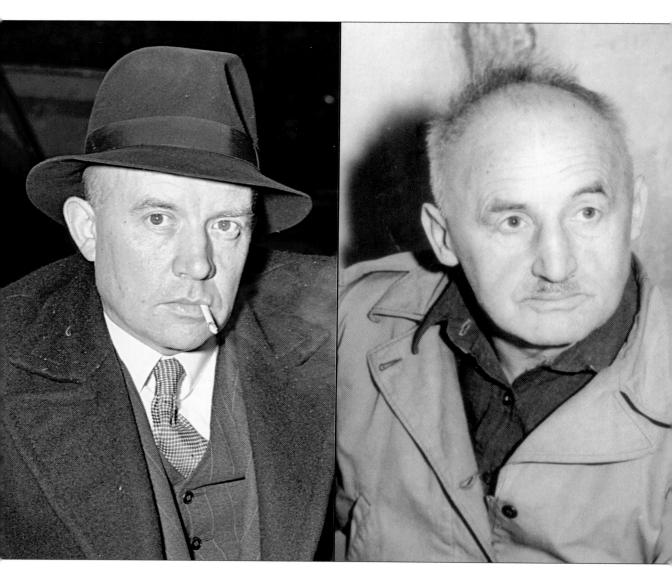

walked in and exclaimed, "Well Dr. Ley, what are you doing here!"[13]

Each week the number of apprehended Nazis grew larger. Alfred Rosenberg, the Nazi philosopher, newspaper publisher, and minister for the Eastern territories, was arrested after he wrote a letter offering his services to the British general Bernard Law Montgomery. After Mont-

gomery's office received Rosenberg's letter, apprehending him was an easy matter; the ex-Nazi ill-advisedly used his real address.

Artur Seyss-Inquart, the Austrian Nazi who terrorized the Dutch people as their governor during the war, was hauled in by the British as he was trying to slip out of the city of Hamburg. The men respon-

leader, a man who poisoned young minds with Nazi ideas, went willingly into captivity just weeks after the last of his boy soldiers died defending a useless bridge in Berlin.

On to the Detention Camps

Arresting the men who helped Hitler was only the first step in bringing the top Nazis to justice. In June and July 1945 the British and Americans began to pool their prisoners. Two separate detention facilities were set up to house the top Nazis until a decision could be made about how to handle them. At that moment there was still some lingering uncertainty whether the men were prisoners of war or war criminals. Prisoners of war would be released, but war criminals faced trial. They needed to be interrogated before their status could be made official. Determining their status was very complicated and a matter for higher authorities than the common soldiers who had actually rounded up Hitler's accomplices. Special teams of experts in war and law had to be

sible for financing Hitler's regime, Walther Funk and Hjalmar Schacht, were captured by American forces. Nazi foreign minister Joachim von Ribbentrop was captured while he was asleep in bed. Carrying only his wash kit and wearing pink and white pajamas, Ribbentrop was taken away to a jail cell. Baldur von Schirach, the half-American Hitler Youth organization

The Great Escapees: Heinrich Himmler

Hitler and Goebbels, hiding deep underground in Berlin, chose to escape capture through death, and Heinrich Himmler eventually followed them. But first he tried to get away with his life. Himmler had been Hitler's favorite killer. As head of the SS, Himmler had been the overlord of the massive system of Nazi concentration and death camps. He was also the architect of the scheme to murder the Jews. Peter Padfield notes in his book *Himmler: A Full-Scale Biography of One of Hitler's Most Ruthless Executioners* that the SS chief stated without reservation that "All Jews we can reach now . . . are to be exterminated without exception."

In early May 1945 Himmler shaved his moustache, put a patch over one eye, and pulled on the uniform of a sergeant in the German secret military police. Disguised, he made an attempt to leave Germany for the Netherlands, hoping to get on a ship bound for South America. While sneaking across northern Germany, Himmler was intercepted by a British patrol on May 21. He was unaware that an arrest order had been issued for men dressed in the uniform he was wearing. Under questioning by his captors, Himmler revealed his true identity. Yet during a lull in the interrogation, he slowly maneuvered a poison capsule, hidden in his mouth, between his teeth. Before the soldiers around him knew what had happened, Himmler bit down on the capsule and fell to the floor. He died within minutes, despite frantic efforts to save him. Like Hitler and Goebbels, Himmler would never face a judge.

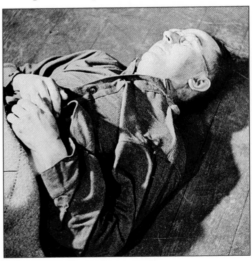

SS chief Heinrich Himmler committed suicide shortly after his capture in May 1945.

assembled and new definitions of war crime needed to be written. Innovative courtroom procedures and practices would have to be developed. Tasks like these would take time. So until the world decided how to handle them, the twenty-two Nazis destined for trial were to be securely put away in a pair of camps (code-named Ashcan and Dustbin) to begin the process of interrogation.

Chapter Two

Interrogations

Arresting major Nazi war criminals was only the start of the long and arduous process of meting out justice to the men who had engineered the Nazi terror, officials in Hitler's government who, in the words of a former concentration camp guard, "were the ones who gave the commands and knew all about it—and could have prevented it."[14] After capture, the logical next step was to find out exactly who these men were in terms of their personalities, what roles they played in the Nazi program, and how they planned to explain their actions. The Allies, hoping to understand the Nazi terror, needed clear portraits of Hitler's elite and a solid historical record of how they would try to justify their crimes. Compiling such a record began with talking to the inmates in the holding cells at the temporary detention centers where they were kept prior to transfer to Nuremberg.

Ashcan and Dustbin

The Nazi leaders captured in the spring of 1945 were collected at two makeshift jails run by the Allied command. The name of each was a sly reference to garbage disposal. The Americans maintained one near the town of Mondorf in Luxembourg; it was code-named Ashcan. The British facility, Dustbin, was located in Germany at Kransberg Castle outside the city of Frankfurt am Main. The Allies determined which camp a Nazi prisoner would be sent to according to the nationality of the soldiers who had captured him.

Serving similar purposes, Ashcan and Dustbin were rather different types of jails. Dustbin was somewhat more comfortable, with good food and a relatively relaxed atmosphere. The prisoners at the British facility could speak freely among themselves and move about the grounds unguarded. There were even cabaret shows and poetry readings at night for the inmates' entertainment.

Rorschach Tests

Developed in 1921 by the psychologist Hermann Rorschach, the tests that bore his name were supposed to reveal the inner workings of the mind via association. The basic procedure involved showing a series of inkblots to the person being examined and asking what they thought they saw. The answers given told the examiner what sorts of thoughts and emotions characterized the person's subconscious.

At Nuremberg sixteen of the twenty-one defendants were given Rorschach tests. The results indicated that the men were plagued by dark moods and had many negative thoughts about life and humanity. The men revealed themselves to be angry, gloomy, and insecure. Fifteen defendants were diagnosed as being depressed; fourteen had violent tendencies. All except one were found to be psychopathic to some extent. Scholars Florence R. Miale and Michael Selzer, in their book *The Nuremberg Mind: The Psychology of the Nazi Leaders*, evaluated the Nuremberg Rorschach tests and concluded that the ex-Nazis on trial "were not psychologically normal or healthy individuals."

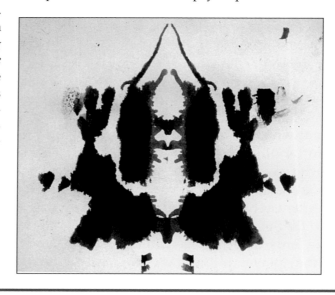

Defendants who were given Rorschach tests told examiners what they saw in inkblots like this one.

Ashcan was quite the opposite. Life there, under the Americans, was far more regimented and unpleasant. The prisoners' rooms, for example, were small and cold, with only a cot and small table and chair for furniture. Three bland meals a day were served, adding up to no more than a mere eighteen hundred calories per prisoner. Göring, who came into captivity at over 250 pounds, lost an average of 2 pounds each week while at Ashcan. By the time of his transfer to Nuremberg none of his clothes fit.

Ashcan was also heavily guarded. Wire fences, one electrified, surrounded the camp. Armed guards in watchtowers had orders to shoot any prisoner who came near the jail's perimeter. Colonel Burton Andrus was the man responsible for their oppressive surroundings. Andrus had no sympathy for the men in his custody. The colonel told one of the interrogators assigned to Ashcan that he would have no trouble with any of the inmates. Andrus said that he "knew how to keep those [criminals] in line." Andrus assured the interrogator that, one way or another, he would "see to it that they would give us the answers we wanted."[15]

The First Questions

The men who had the job of questioning the prisoners were assigned to the Field Intelligence Agency Technical (FIAT) and the Combined Intelligence Objectives Subcommittee (CIOS). At this early stage the questioning was not tied to the judicial process; rather, the interrogations at Ashcan had been designed to collect raw information on Nazi German science, industry, technology, and economics during the war. The material FIAT and CIOS gathered would have no immediate value in a courtroom. For this reason, despite Andrus's encouragement to be hard, the interrogation tended to be relaxed and sometimes informal. One interrogator was so polite to his subjects that a colleague asked angrily, "Do you think this is a football game we have been through[?] . . . Are we supposed to shake hands and just treat them like good sports?"[16]

Göring found the good treatment he received in the interrogating room to be laughable. Göring remembered how the Nazis had tortured their prisoners; the Americans, he felt, were too soft. He even once scolded a questioner saying, "Captain, you don't do this right. If we had won, we wouldn't have it done this way— you'd be standing up, and you wouldn't have your uniform on, you'd have a black and white prisoner's suit, and there would be two SS men standing behind you, sticking you in the butt with bayonets. . . . That's the way you ought to treat us."[17] Göring was almost insulted by the smiles and easy treatment he was given. A leader of his stature, Göring felt, should be questioned more formally about matters of state policy. He would get his wish at the central prison in Nuremberg.

The Next Stop

On August 5, 1945, the supreme Allied commander, General Dwight D. Eisenhower, ordered the transfer of top Nazis from their temporary holding camps to the prison at Nuremberg. The switch took place quickly. Within ten days the Nazi prisoners were assembled and ready for further interrogations, even though Hess had not arrived from England, and Fritsche and Raeder had not been flown in from Russia.

The officer in charge of the questioning was Colonel John Harlan Amen, chief of the U.S. Army's interrogation division. An experienced lawyer, Amen was selected for duty at Nuremberg because of his legal skills and organizational ability. Colonel Amen had available all the tools and manpower he would need to conduct thorough interrogations of the prisoners.

A hardworking team of researchers at the documents division assisted him. Their

As preparations for the trials proceeded, the prisoners were transferred to the Nuremberg Jail.

job was to collate and analyze the reams of German documents seized after the war. The Nazis had kept meticulous records of their activities, some so incriminating that the American analysts could hardly believe it. "The documentary evidence," one researcher wrote, "is just unbelievable. Their own reports illustrated with pictures . . . on the persecution of the Jews, crimes against humanity, etc. The Germans certainly believed in putting everything in writing."[18]

Armed with piles of German orders, official letters, lists, accounting records, and government reports, Amen prepared to go to work. His counterparts from Britain, France, and Russia did the same.

The Preliminaries

Even before conducting the first official interrogations, Amen ordered that a series of sophisticated psychological and medical tests be performed on the Nuremberg inmates. Prison doctors and psychiatrists, led by U.S. Army majors Douglas Kelly and John K. Lattimer, wrote physical and psychological profiles of each man. In terms of health, the prisoners were relatively well. Göring had lost weight and been cured of his drug addiction, but Funk had bladder and heart problems. The vain Göring, in fact, was perhaps one of the fittest inmates. One Nuremberg doctor later wrote that "he was far better off physically [than before], and made a much better appearance, all of which flattered him."[19]

The team also conducted intelligence tests that demonstrated that all of the prisoners possessed above average mental capabilities. They discovered that the highest IQ belonged to former finance minister Schacht (143), while the lowest was that of the racist publisher Julius Streicher (106). A series of Rorschach inkblot tests showed that although some of the men were emotionally unbalanced, none of them were legally insane. According to the tests, all of the men at Nuremberg were fit to stand trial.

Asking Questions: Hermann Göring

With all the initial preparations completed, Amen and his men began asking questions in a manner far different from that at Ashcan. The character of the pretrial interrogations at Nuremberg was established early and was tailored to fit the men being interviewed. The twenty-two prisoners to be questioned were different kinds of people. Some were quiet and very proper; others were loud, arrogant, and defiant. To get the most information, each man had to be approached in a unique way. Despite their individuality, the men's responses under interrogation were eerily similar.

From the start, most of the prisoners tried either to deny responsibility for their actions or to shift blame to Hitler and Himmler, both of whom were conveniently dead. Only Göring acknowledged his role; in fact, he defended it. Despite being labeled "one of the world's worst criminals"[20] by his cap-

tors, Göring acted as if he had done nothing wrong. Hitler's number-two man never denied his part in the Nazi plan. He freely admitted that he helped expand and maintain the Nazi system and saw nothing wrong with Hitler's goals. Göring had trouble at times even understanding why

During his interrogation, Hermann Göring (shown here shortly after his capture) showed no remorse for his role in the Nazi horror.

he was in jail: "What am I doing here any-way?"[21] he once asked his jailors.

Throughout the Göring sessions, the interrogators could never seem to extract from him the slightest bit of remorse or regret. Göring was, in the words of one officer's report, "neither stupid nor a fool . . . but generally cool and calculating."[22] As the interrogations proceeded, Göring continued to use his obvious intelligence to throw off his questioners and thus to shield himself from the criminal charges leveled against him.

Asking Questions: Rudolf Hess

Hess denied his responsibility outright; indeed, he denied any memory at all of his Nazi past. Hess had been complaining of amnesia since his days in a British jail. He also displayed signs of mental illness. The amnesia was at one point tentatively confirmed, but Hess's sanity was never in doubt. Many experts, then and since, questioned whether Hitler's one-time deputy was genuinely afflicted or merely faking. Some say it was for real, others that it was simply an elaborate ruse designed to allow Hess to evade the law. Whatever the case, interrogating Hess proved frustrating and often useless.

After a few attempts at direct questioning failed, Hess's interrogators tried some shock tactics. When Hess argued that he could not remember anything about his time in Hitler's service, Amen confronted him with his former colleague, Göring. Together for the first time since 1941, Göring and Hess sat across from one another. In his book *Interrogations: The Nazi*

Elite in Allied Hands, historian Richard Overy quotes the official transcript in his account of this conversation.

> "Listen, Hess, I was the Supreme Commander of the Luftwaffe, and you flew to England in one of my planes. Don't you remember . . . don't you remember?" Göring said.
>
> "No," Hess replied flatly.
>
> "Don't you remember I was made Reichsmarshal at a meeting of the Reichstag [the German parliament] while you were present?"
>
> "No," Hess said again.
>
> "Do you remember that the Führer . . . announced in the Reichstag that if something happened to him, that I would be his successor, and if something happened to me, you were to be my successor? Don't you remember that?" Göring asked, his frustration building.
>
> "No," Hess repeated. "No; that is all black. That is all black. That is all blacked out."
>
> Göring sighed, "I have come to the end. I cannot ask him any more."

In the former Luftwaffe chief's opinion, Hess was "completely crazy."[23]

Later attempts at questioning Hess proved even less productive. Only once did he hint that he might remember more

When questioned, Rudolf Hess steadfastly claimed to have no memory of his involvement in the Nazis' crimes.

than he was letting on. During a brief session together Amen asked Hess whether he thought Göring was a criminal; Hess said that he did. When Amen asked why he thought that, Hess responded that he knew because he was the same type of criminal. Immediately sensing that he had admitted too much, Hess became quiet and never mentioned anything about crime again.

The Other Prisoners Talk

Göring denied having done anything wrong; Hess said he could not remember his Nazi past. The other men being interrogated at Nuremberg fell somewhere

John Harlan Amen: Interrogation Leader

Colonel John Harlan Amen, chief of Interrogation Division, had been a New York lawyer before World War II. He had a distinguished record of prosecuting corruption and racketeering cases, especially ones that involved elaborate conspiracies. Amen had also served on the staff of the U.S. Attorney General. Amen's experience suited him well for the task of questioning and gathering evidence from men involved in history's largest criminal conspiracy. Amen looked forward to the challenge of interrogating such infamous figures as the prisoners at Nuremberg. He volunteered, in fact, to be the sole interrogator of the toughest of the group—Göring, Kaltenbrunner, and Otto Ohlendorf. Amen's desire to see justice done extended into the courtroom, where he served under Robert H. Jackson as an assistant prosecutor.

between these two points. They claimed little if any knowledge of the persecution of the Jews and accepted only a small part of the responsibility for what was done in Hitler's name. Von Papen, Hitler's vice-chancellor for a brief time, acknowledged his role in bringing the Nazis to power but denied having ever supported their policies. Speer not only denied helping Hitler, he portrayed himself as someone who evolved into an anti-Nazi and actually plotted to kill Hitler. Frick, the ex-minister of the interior, admitted that he oversaw the German police but said that he bore no responsibility for the arrests they made. "[People] were arrested," Frick claimed, "but they were not arrested by me and they were arrested without [my] knowledge."[24]

One after another the Nuremberg prisoners proclaimed their ignorance and innocence. No one, it seemed, had had anything to do with the oppressive poli-

cies of Hitler and the Nazi Party. Funk, the ex-Nazi finance minister and head of the Reichsbank, answered each question put to him by restating his total ignorance of what his own government agency was up to. He argued that he had no idea where all the gold kept in his vaults came from and knew nothing about the secret Nazi bank accounts in Switzerland. Von Ribbentrop told his interrogator that he had nothing whatsoever to do with Hitler's murder program. He denied any knowledge of what was being done to the Jews. In fact, von Ribbentrop protested that such a thing was really quite impossible.

Perhaps the most unbelievable denial came from Frank. Frank was the governor of Poland at a time when millions of Jews were being shot, gassed, and starved to death. Frank told his interrogators that he knew nothing about the death camps, even though they were located within his area of administration and he occasionally passed by them in his official travels. Frank contended that despite numerous reports and meetings about every detail of life in Poland, he was unaware that Jews were being sent by the trainload to die in his domain. Just because he ruled Poland for years, Frank argued, that "was no reason why I should know everything that happened."[25]

Handing Down the Indictments

The parade of denials continued until the interrogations came to an abrupt end on October 19, 1945. That day the twenty-two men at Nuremberg were formally indicted for crimes committed during the Nazi years. Each prisoner now officially became a defendant in a criminal case. As such, according to American and British law, they were no longer required to submit to interrogations. Göring and Speer chose to continue meeting with Allied interrogators, but most of the other defendants decided to remain silent until they could meet with their new lawyers.

The day that the indictments came down, the accused reacted almost exclusively with a combination of fear and worry. Some looked forward to getting a chance to explain themselves; others were nervous about what a trial might reveal. Only Ley, the former labor minister, lashed out at his jailors. While being informed of the charges against him, Ley screamed that he could not understand why the soldiers did not just shoot the defendants on the spot, rather than subject them to the humiliation of a trial. "Stand us up against the wall and shoot us! You are the victors!" Ley yelled. Some hours later, Ley sat down in his cell and wrote a letter to his lawyer saying, "I was anti-semitic, I admit, but is this a crime [?] . . . I am no criminal."[26]

Soon afterward Ley tore a few strips from his prison towel and soaked them in water to make them easier to knot. After tying them together, Ley tied one end of the waterlogged strips to a pipe over the toilet and the other around his neck and strangled himself. Ley would not accompany his codefendants into the courtroom on November 20, the date the International Military Tribunal had decreed their trial would begin.

Chapter Three

Prosecutors, Defenders, and Judges

The crimes committed by the Nazis had no equals in history. Never before had the world confronted persecution, torture, and murder on such a large scale. The offenses committed by the Nazi Germans required not only the establishment of the greatest international tribunal ever called, but also the development of new legal procedures. In fact, the word "crime" itself was redefined. Novel tools and methods were created and used by both the prosecution and the defense at Nuremberg. Both sides had much to learn and do as each sought justice for the accused and for their victims.

Building the Prosecution

The prosecuting attorneys began gathering in Nuremberg at the end of May 1945, even as top Nazis were still being arrested. Arriving early, the Americans were eager to put together a case against the defendants. The British, who joined them, were content to let their American coun-

terparts, who seemed better prepared, take the lead. The Russian and French contingents, for their part, were slow to assemble and proved to be much more disorganized. It became evident that even though the prosecution was supposed to consist of equals, it was primarily an American-led effort. One American lawyer, in fact, predicted that the proceedings would follow a simple script: "The United States tries the whole . . . case and the other nations make some speeches and offer supplemental evidence."[27]

The sheer number of Americans at Nuremberg, if nothing else, dictated a commanding role in the prosecution. A total of 640 American experts, technicians, and lawyers descended on the city. The British sent only 168; the French and the Russians provided a mere 80 staff members between them. Heading the American entourage was Supreme Court justice Robert H. Jackson. An aggressive and confident attorney, Jackson was a former U.S.

attorney general, picked because of his reputation for tenacity in and out of the courtroom. A battery of talented military and civilian lawyers, including Colonel Robert G. Storey, Thomas J. Dodd, and Brigadier General Telford Taylor, among others, assisted Jackson. Sir David Maxwell-Fyfe of Great Britain, France's François de Menthon, and Russia's General Roman Rudenko also joined Jackson in Nuremberg. They were all experienced attorneys who would prove their skills in

Robert H. Jackson: Chief Prosecutor

The chief American prosecutor at Nuremberg, Robert H. Jackson, was born in Pennsylvania in February 1892 and was raised in New York. Oddly, given his later prominence, Jackson never went to college beyond a one-year course of study at a New York law school; he apprenticed with a practicing lawyer until he qualified for the bar in 1913. Twenty years later Jackson made his way to Washington, D.C., where he became a legal counsel at the U.S. Treasury. He worked his way up from there to be an assistant attorney general, and finally U.S. attorney general under President Franklin Delano Roosevelt.

In June 1941 Roosevelt nominated Jackson for the Supreme Court; he was confirmed in less than one month. Jackson served as a justice for four years before being asked to take the position at the head of the American prosecution at Nuremberg. After the successful conclusion of the trials in September 1946, Jackson returned to the United States and his seat on the Supreme Court. He served as a justice for eight more years until his death in October 1954.

Robert H. Jackson (standing at the podium) was chosen to head the American prosecution team because of his reputation for tenacity in the courtroom.

Sir David Maxwell-Fyfe, Thomas J. Dodd, Brigadier General Telford Taylor, and General Roman Rudenko (left to right) assisted in the prosecution at Nuremberg.

the months to come, but Jackson was clearly the chief.

Jackson's Case

The prosecution had at its disposal a virtual mountain of evidence against the Nuremberg defendants. The documentary evidence alone was overwhelming. The load of papers pertaining to the SS, for example, filled six railroad freight cars. Taken together, the Allies had confiscated 5 million typewritten pages. The size of the cache and its value against the defendants prompted Jackson to comment once that he "did not think men would be so foolish as to put in writing some of the things the Germans did. The stupidity of it and the brutality would simply appall you."[28] Thousands of feet of film footage was added to this incriminating record, as was the sworn testimony of eyewitnesses.

The prosecution built a solid and innovative case on this substantial foundation. Jackson's strategy was to try not only specific war criminals but also entire Nazi organizations. No one had ever attempted to attach guilt to whole groups of people regardless of individual actions. Personal responsibility, according to precedent, was what mattered. Now simply

being a member of an indicted organization might make one guilty of crimes up to and including murder. The "criminal gangs,"[29] as the Russians called them, indicted at Nuremberg included the SS, the Gestapo, the *Wehrmacht* (armed forces) high command, and the Nazi Party Leadership Corps. These groups, in Jackson's opinion, were perhaps even more to blame for the Nazi terror than the individual defendants. "It would be a greater catastrophe," he argued, "to acquit these organizations than it would be to acquit . . . the defendants in the box."[30]

The prosecution charged the organizations with being at the center of a vast and murderous criminal conspiracy. They, along with the men in the dock, were indicted on four separate counts. Count One stated that the Nazi Party and the defendants conspired to wage aggressive war and "carried out this common plan or conspiracy in ruthless and complete disregard and violation of the laws of humanity." Count Two brought the charge of general crimes against world peace. The third count accused the defendants of explicit war crimes. It stated that the Nazis "murdered and tortured civilians . . . and imprisoned them without legal process."[31] The summary execution of Allied prisoners of war and the abuse of slave laborers were included under Count Three of the indictment.

Arguably the most serious charges were detailed in the fourth count—crimes against humanity. Here it was contended that the Nazi organizations and the twenty-one defendants had a common purpose of murdering their enemies, namely the Jews. The count held that the men at Nuremberg had participated in a program through which "millions of Jews from Germany and the occupied Western Countries were sent to Eastern Countries for extermination."[32]

Reactions to the indictments varied from man to man. Von Ribbentrop protest-ed that the charges were "directed against the wrong people." Dönitz laughed them off as nothing more than "typical American humor."[33] Yet the indictments handed down by the International Military Tribunal contained serious accusations. Jackson and the other Allied prosecutors, however, still needed all the evidence they could gather if they hoped to convict the men and organizations on trial. Documents and films certainly helped, but the

The men selected to represent the accused war criminals at Nuremberg were all experienced lawyers but they lacked the knowledge necessary to mount an aggressive defense.

truly convincing evidence would come from the witnesses, perpetrators and victims alike, who were prepared to testify.

Defending the Indefensible

Given the amount and type of evidence, the defense attorneys at Nuremberg faced a difficult task. To begin with, the men they would represent did not even agree on the need for any counsel at all. Indeed, Taylor recalled that "some were unable or unwilling to take it seriously . . . [others] took the matter of counsel very seriously."[34] Once they had been appointed, the lawyers would have to prove that their clients were not guilty, at least not guilty of the specific charges leveled against them, despite all of the evidence against them.

The defendants chose their lawyers primarily from a list provided to them by the tribunal. Frank, Kaltenbrunner, and Frick all had legal backgrounds, but they could not very well help their comrades while on trial themselves, so they chose counsel. Göring accepted a lawyer recommended by the British prosecutor. Dönitz made a specific request that the tribunal quickly granted. He wanted a "submarine admiral to come here to defend me. You see," Dönitz reasoned, "he can understand me. He did the same job."[35] He was assigned a former naval judge as his attorney.

In all, forty-eight lawyers were eventually chosen to participate in the defense, of which only eight had any criminal trial experience. Eighteen had been Nazi party members themselves, but their membership had been inactive and was used only

to retain their positions on the bench. The remaining attorneys had all been dedicated anti-Nazis. The defense team, thus, had little firsthand knowledge of the kind necessary to mount aggressive cases and even less sympathy for the men on trial.

The defense's job was made even more challenging by the restrictions imposed on the lawyers by the authorities. To begin with, the defense could rely on neither a "just following orders" defense nor on tu quoque ("I did it, but you did the same thing") arguments. This meant that even if someone had been ordered to commit crimes, obedience did not lift the burden of responsibility; it also did not matter if the victorious governments and militaries had taken the same actions. The defense, moreover, had strictly limited access to relevant documents and no staff to help sort and analyze those documents it did obtain. Defense lawyers also could not use Allied war files as they prepared their cases nor could they travel in order to gather witnesses. The Allies claimed that security concerns made such restrictions necessary. Lastly, the defense had only one month to get ready before the beginning of the trial in November.

The attorneys for the accused men, being trained in German law, were also unfamiliar with the Anglo-American style of courtroom proceedings. The German system had the lawyers and judges working together to discover the truth. The defense lawyers did not know how to argue in front of a judge against the prosecutors, something called the adversarial system. They did not even know how to cross-examine a witness properly.

The defense attorneys had other obstacles to overcome outside of the courtroom. The Allied soldiers who guarded the Palace of Justice, the site of the trials, insulted the lawyers routinely and occasionally subjected them to unnecessarily rough searches as they entered the building. The German press attacked the men relentlessly for having the nerve to give their services to Nazi criminals.

Compounding these problems was the controversy over compensation. German lawyers in the 1940s usually made between $7,500 and $10,000 per year. The tribunal at first refused to pay the men anything near this sum. The American lead judge, Francis Biddle, however, reminded his colleagues that it would "be very difficult to find lawyers who will be willing to defend these men unless the tribunal pays [a respectable fee]"[36] for their time. The court finally relented and agreed to provide the defense lawyers with a base salary of $1000 plus $625 per month. The pay was reasonable, but the defense team would have to work very hard to earn it.

The Men Who Would Judge

Hard work would also be required from the men selected to hear and judge the cases against the Nuremberg defendants. No judge had ever presided over these kinds of trials; therefore, each decision would set a new precedent. Drawn even-

Choosing Nuremberg

Several factors influenced the decision to hold the war crimes trials in the city of Nuremberg. For one thing, the facilities at the Palace of Justice were perhaps the best in Germany in 1945. The building was intact, large, and modern enough to host such an important proceeding. Nuremberg also was squarely in the American zone of occupation, a fact that guaranteed good security and services—at American expense. Holding the trials in the American zone also reduced the influence of the Russians at a time when tensions between the Soviet Union and the West were growing.

Perhaps of the greatest importance, however, was Nuremberg's symbolic value. Nuremberg had been known as Hitler's city. It occupied a special place in the culture and mystique of Nazi Germany. During the 1930s the Nazi Party held its massive annual rallies there. These grand political spectacles were designed to convince the German public of the Nazi Party's awesome power. It was also in this city that the infamous 1935 anti-Jewish codes, the Nuremberg Laws, were enacted. Symbolically speaking, no better location in Germany could have been found in which to reveal Hitler's crimes and punish his henchmen.

The Russian and American judges (left to right) A. F. Volchkov, Francis Biddle, General I. T. Nikitchenko, and John Parker, along with two British and two French judges, presided over the Nuremberg Trials.

ly from each of the victorious powers, the judges, while charting new courses in international law, had to see that the accused received a fair trial. The definition of murder, for example, had to be rewritten in order to cover millions of victims killed by different means, at different times, and in different places. The charge of conspiracy had to be reworked to include people who did not know, but should have known, that crimes were being committed. Additionally, the Nuremberg judges had to revise existing notions of international theft and the prevailing rules of war. The judges, in other words, had to make history and at the same time hold speedy trials that avoided even the slightest appearance of vengefulness. The Nuremberg tribunal needed to ensure that a first-of-its-kind trial did not, in the words of historian Robert Conot, "turn into a charade of expediency and retribution rather than a search for the truth."[37]

This was admittedly a heavy burden to be carried by the Allied judges who arrived in Germany through the early fall of 1945. Each Allied government sent two judges to preside at Nuremberg, a primary and one alternate. The American contingent was led by Biddle, a former attorney general who was competent but not well liked by the president at the time, Harry S. Truman. Still, Truman recognized qualities in Biddle that suited him for the task of seeing justice done at Nuremberg. Biddle's alternate, John Parker, was likewise not a Truman favorite but similarly well qualified. Parker, feeling bound by duty to serve his country, accepted his mission with such reluctance that, on the eve of leaving for Europe, he said, "I have never taken a journey for which I had less enthusiasm."[38]

The British representatives on the bench were more positive about their tasks. Lord Chief Justice Geoffrey Lawrence was the primary; Norman Birkett, a seasoned trial lawyer, was selected as the alternate. Lawrence's credentials were such that he was chosen by his colleagues to serve as the president of the court, even though Biddle felt he himself should be in charge. The court president's leading role was also deeply resented by Birkett, who felt himself to be the victim of petty snobbishness in being subordinated to Lawrence.

The bench was completed with the addition of French judges Donnedieu de Vabres and Robert Falco and Russian judges Major General I.T. Nikitchenko and A.F. Volchkov. Volchkov was a longtime prosecutor and criminal judge who favored the type of trial the other Allied judges wanted. Nikitchenko, on the other hand, sought only to mete out punishment to men he felt were already guilty. "We are dealing here," the general said, "with war criminals who have already been convicted."[39] Still, the fiery Russian commander promised to curb his desire for revenge if it might mean seeing the defendants hang.

A Courtroom like No Other

By the end of November 1945 the prosecution and defense teams were prepared to argue their sides, and the judges were ready to hear the cases. The stage for this international drama, the courtroom itself, was also ready.

The city of Nuremberg, selected by the tribunal in part because it had been Hitler's favorite city, had been nearly leveled by American bombers in April of 1945. The venue for the war crimes' trials had been one of the few buildings to sustain only light damage in a thoroughly blasted city center. Most other structures had been gutted or destroyed altogether. Half of the population had streamed out of the ruins as refugees, and twenty thousand of their neighbors lay buried under the rubble at the war's end. An American prosecution staff member described Nuremberg as being the "monumental wreckage of insolent wickedness brought crumbling down on the heads of the wrongdoers. . . . The city smells of broken pipes and shattered masonry and here and there corpses not yet disinterred. [The citizens] have come out of the teachings of death into its realization."[40]

Somehow, though, the Palace of Justice and its attached prison had survived. The actual room where the trial would be held at one time housed a Nazi court so it had to be completely remodeled. The renovation, carried out by skilled workmen assisted by SS and German army prisoners of war, included new wiring for cameras,

Technology in the Courtroom

The technology showcased at Nuremberg made the trials thoroughly modern proceedings. The courtroom was filled with still cameras, motion picture cameras, film projectors, recording devices, and radio broadcasting equipment. Arguably the most significant piece of hardware on display was the IBM voice translation system. Fully automated and provided to the International Military Tribunal free of charge, the IBM network made the trial process more efficient, and also more just, by allowing for a proper and complete understanding of the testimony being offered. The equipment was operated by a total of 108 men and women—specialized interpreters, general translators, secretaries, and stenographers backed by a large staff of technicians.

The machinery itself was complex and very sophisticated. Everyone in the courtroom, except the guards, wore headphones that connected them to the translators through a mass of spaghettilike wires that spread across the courtroom floor. The translators themselves sat in a large glass booth nicknamed "the aquarium." Here they followed the proceedings and produced their translations, which were sent out via a five-channel broadcast array. The trial participants thus had reliable real-time translations available at any time, courtesy of the IBM Corporation.

lighting, and the powerful IBM simultaneous translation system. The IBM machines were designed to provide five channels of ongoing translation to every person in the courtroom.

A special elevator was also installed and covered passageways constructed in order to transfer safely the defendants from their cells to the courtroom. Defendants' docks and spectators' galleries were built, as were tables for the small army of court reporters and secretaries. Special glass cubicles were erected for the translators to work in. Finally, a witness box was constructed and placed next to a huge movie screen, installed so the court could view films of Nazi crimes.

The refurbished courtroom was a masterpiece of cutting-edge technology, designed as a fitting place to hold history's greatest trial. Beginning on November 20, 1945, the courtroom's modern machines and gadgets would help the world see and hear the record of a murderous regime.

Chapter Four

The Prosecution Opens

The indictments handed down in October 1945 charged the men at Nuremberg with enormous, hideous crimes. The accusations held them responsible for repression, injustice, and cold-blooded murder on a continental scale. With the massive amount of evidence arrayed against them, the guilt of Göring and the others seemed self-evident, and convictions seemed like a foregone conclusion. But this was still a trial, and the legal process required that Jackson's team of prosecutors prove its case beyond a reasonable doubt.

Jackson Before the Bench

On November 20, 1945, the defendants were led from their cells into the newly renovated courtroom to make their pleas. Each man was scheduled to come before the judges and declare his guilt or innocence concerning the charges against him. The only defendant not in attendance that day was former SD chief Kaltenbrunner.

He spent the time in a hospital bed, having suffered a ruptured blood vessel in his head two days earlier. The other defendants had the indictments reread to them in separate morning and afternoon sessions. During the lunch break the defendants pretended to be upbeat, but as they returned to the courtroom, former Hitler Youth organizer von Schirach said to the prison psychologist, Gustave Gilbert, "This is a bad day—not for you, but for us."[41] At the end of the day the men were taken back to the prison, where they waited for the actual trial to begin.

The next day the defendants, whom Biddle later described as "drab men once great"[42] and who seemed not to realize the pain their loyalty to Hitler had brought to Europe, were asked how they pleaded; each responded in the same way—not guilty. Following their pleas the men sat for the most part expressionless as Jackson approached the microphone in the middle of the courtroom. He arranged his notes and then opened the prosecution by reiterating the enormity of the crimes committed by the Nazis in general and the defendants in particular. Jackson told the tribunal:

> The wrongs which we seek to condemn and punish have been so calculated, so malignant, and so devastating, that civilization cannot tolerate their being ignored. . . . In the prisoners dock sit twenty-odd broken men . . . these prisoners represent sinister influences that will lurk in the world long after their bodies have returned to dust. We will show them to be living symbols of racial hatreds, of terrorism and violence, and of the arrogance and cruelty of power.[43]

Eight judges (back row)—two each from the United States, the Soviet Union, Britain, and France—preside at the opening of the Nuremberg Trials.

Emphasizing his point, Jackson said that the prosecution sought not only to reveal the extent of the Nazi criminal conspiracy but also to bring its creators to justice. The chief prosecutor explained that while it was important to punish everyone responsible for putting Hitler's program into action, he was after the ringleaders. The prosecution, Jackson stated, was determined to call to account the "men who knew how to use lesser folk as tools . . . the planners and designers, the inciters and leaders"[44] of a lethal criminal enterprise.

The Crimes and the Case

Jackson's powerful opening statement was the high point of a prosecution strategy that, early on, almost led to disaster. After what Birkett hailed as "a very fine open-ing speech,"[45] the staff prosecutors took turns detailing the history of Nazi criminality. They offered narratives that covered the entire time of Nazi rule, from 1933 to 1945. What Jackson's people hoped to reveal was a tale of a conspiracy so broad that it implicated each of the defendants at some point. Combining chronology with the documentary evidence, Jackson sought to prove the guilt of all of the defendants at once.

It was an ambitious but flawed plan. The judges, spectators, and accused listened dutifully, but after eight days most people in the courtroom were becoming bored. The judges fidgeted in their seats, while some of the defendants busied themselves either by taking notes as Keitel and Jodl did, or by switching between

Aktion Reinhard

Named after the SS general Reinhard Heydrich, who was assassinated in Czechoslovakia in May 1942, *Aktion Reinhard* was the code name given to the overall plan to wipe out Europe's Jews in factorylike camps located in Poland. The plan, developed by Heydrich under orders from Hitler and Himmler, was complicated and would eventually involve many different agencies of the Nazi government in an effort to kill a total of 11 million Jews through the use of poison gas.

The Nazis considered the shooting operations of the SS *Einsatzgruppen* to be a success. Mass shootings, however, proved too slow and too psychologically stressful from the German perspective. A cleaner, faster method that was easier on the killers' consciences had to be found, the Nazis thought. The decision was made, therefore, in the summer of 1941, to switch from guns to poisonous carbon monoxide gas and a new cyanide gas known as Zyklon B. These gasses were to be fed into specially designed chambers where hundreds of people at a time could be murdered. From 1942 to 1944 the camps set up under *Aktion Reinhard* gassed over 3 million innocent Jews.

As part of its presentation the prosecution displayed a map showing the locations of Nazi concentration camps.

language channels like von Papen. Hess sat through the opening days with a book open in front of him, the pages of which he never turned. The only real excitement was generated by Göring, who responded to every statement made by a prosecutor with elaborate, even comical, gestures. Jackson, aware that he was losing his hold over the audience, acknowledged to the court that "I am aware . . . that the material I am pursuing is a little tedious."[46]

The prosecution needed to get back on track and regain the initiative by reminding the tribunal how horrible the Nazi crimes had been. To do that, Jackson decided to bring out and use a shocking visual aid. Graphic images might succeed where words seemed to be failing. Jackson asked the court for permission to show a film cataloging Nazi atrocities in the concentration camps.

This new and aggressive tactic worked better than any of the prosecutors could have imagined. As the lights dimmed and the film began to flicker on the courtroom's huge screen, gasps could be heard. The movie stunned the audience and forced the defendants to confront the human costs of their actions. Funk sat in his seat crying throughout the showing; von Ribbentrop refused to look. Von Schirach shuddered; Schacht fumed and demanded to know why he was being forced to sit with criminals and watch such a disgusting movie. Even the defense attorneys muttered, "for God's sake—terrible."[47]

Only Göring seemed to have remained unmoved by the scenes of battered camp inmates and mounds of twisted corpses. He had spent the afternoon ignoring the film, looking around the courtroom. After all he had seen, Göring's only complaint was that the film had ruined his whole day. "It was such a good afternoon, too," he said mockingly, "and then they showed . . . that awful film, and it just spoiled everything!"[48]

Enter the British

Jackson moved quickly to capitalize on the effects of the atrocity film. He called the Americans' first witness to the stand, a general whose testimony was dramatic but less than damaging. The defense attorneys did a good job during cross-examination. Overall, the prosecution under the Americans had moved steadily forward. When the British joined in, however, the momentum increased. Sir Hartley Shawcross opened the British case in strong, clear words. He accused the defendants of being the driving force behind the Nazi terror. They had been, in his words,

> the instruments without which Hitler's will could not be carried out; and they were more than that. These men were no mere willing tools, although they would be guilty enough if that has been their role. They are the men whose support built Hitler up into the position of power he occupied; these are the men whose initiative and planning often conceived and certainly made possible the acts of aggression done in Hitler's name. . . . They are the men whose cooperation and support made the Nazi Government of Germany possible.[49]

Shawcross concluded by lashing out at the men in the dock, calling them arrogant and cunning criminals who tried to set themselves up as the leaders of what they imagined to be a master race.

Energized by Shawcross's eloquent and stirring description of the accused as Hitler's accomplices, the Americans kept up the momentum by showing another atrocity film. This one, entitled *The Nazi Plan*, was even more gruesome than the first. Next, Jackson offered reams of documents detailing Nazi efforts to murder systematically those people the Nazis deemed to be inferior. Finally, Jackson showed an amateur movie of SS men killing Jews and then using human body parts as trophies. Von Schirach, devastated by what he saw, remarked later that after what the judges had seen, "I wouldn't blame the court if they just said, 'Chop off all their heads!'"[50]

The defense lawyers had no way to refute what they and everyone else in the courtroom had seen with their own eyes. The Nazi crimes were undeniable and certainly indefensible. The defense was shaken by the force of the prosecution's evidence and the aggressive posture of Jackson, Shawcross, and their colleagues. Unsure what to do next, the defense decided to ask for a recess over the Christmas holidays in order to regroup and come up with some strategy to counter the prosecution.

Jackson, having gained the upper hand, objected vigorously. He did not want to let up the pressure or give the defendants and their attorneys time to collect themselves. Tribunal president Lawrence, however, saw things differently. "In a trial of this complexity and magnitude," he said, "the tribunal considers that it is not only in the interests of the defendants and their counsel but of everyone concerned in the trial that there should be a recess."[51] He overruled Jackson and declared the court adjourned from December 20, 1945 through January 2, 1946.

The Trial Resumes

The defendants came back into the courtroom on January 3. Their attorneys had

The Commando Order of 1942

The order issued by Adolf Hitler calling for the summary execution of captured Allied commandos was a key piece of evidence against the German high command at Nuremberg. Issued after the disastrous Canadian raid on the French port city of Dieppe in August 1942, the order told German soldiers to kill uniformed commandos taken prisoner, even if they were unarmed. Drawn up with the knowledge of Wilhelm Keitel and Alfred Jodl, the directive was a perfect example of the types of criminal orders given to the German armed forces during World War II. As recorded in Eugene Davidson's book, *The Trial of the Germans*, Hitler's order stated that "all enemies on so-called Commando missions . . . even if they are to all appearances soldiers in uniform . . . whether armed or unarmed . . . are to be slaughtered to the last man." Grand Admiral Erich Raeder reiterated the command for the German navy.

Military law holds that combatants in uniform who surrender are to be confined safely after being taken into custody. Killing such prisoners is expressly forbidden. The Commando Order thus implicated the German military in acts that could only be called murder.

hoped to collect themselves sufficiently during the recess to respond to the prosecution's attacks. The defense had been hurt badly by the witnesses, documents, and especially the films offered by Jackson's team. Only on rare occasions had cross-examination done any good; the evidence was simply too strong.

The prosecution without a doubt had gained firm control of the proceedings. Now Jackson and his colleagues, sensing their command, returned to the cases with renewed intensity. Rested and rejuvenated, the prosecution began presenting sworn affidavits from former SS killers and in some instances brought the killers themselves into the courtroom to tell their stories. Their testimony in one way or another implicated each defendant.

Perhaps the most notorious of the SS executioners to appear in court was Otto Ohlendorf, the man who had commanded the special action group (*Einsatzgruppe* D) assigned to kill the Jews in southern Russia. Praised by Himmler as Nazism's "Knight of the Holy Grail"[52] in reference to King Arthur's loyal men who would do anything in their master's service, Ohlendorf followed every order, even if it told him to commit murder. Ohlendorf had, in fact, ruthlessly annihilated tens of thousands of innocent people, and he readily admitted this during an interview. Ohlendorf acknowledged his responsibility for his crimes but claimed that since he did not actually pull the trigger, he bore no personal responsibility.

On the stand Ohlendorf testified that the entire Nazi leadership knew all about the mass shooting operations that he supervised in Russia. Everyone knew very well what was happening, he said, and that included the men on trial. Ohlendorf specially singled out Frank, Rosenberg, Speer, Saukel, Kaltenbrunner's SS, and the army high command as guilty parties. The witnesses who followed him implicated these men as well as Funk and Göring.

Some of the most damaging testimony came from top SS leaders such as Erich von dem Bach-Zelewski, the SS officer responsible for central Russia, and Dieter Wisliceny, aide to Adolf Eichmann, the SS officer in charge of killing the Jews. Bach-Zelewski's words, in particular, struck so hard that Göring exploded in rage. "Why, that dirty, bloody, treacherous swine!" Göring screamed during a break in the trial, "[Bach-Zelewski] was the bloodiest murderer of the whole . . . set up. The dirty, filthy *Schweinhund*, selling his soul to save his stinking neck!"[53] Wisliceny confirmed for the tribunal that all of Hitler's closest officers and advisers knew of his plans regarding the Jews and anyone else deemed unfit by Nazi standards. The court also heard from a former death camp commander. The sworn testimony of Rudolf Höss, the top Nazi at Auschwitz, pointed out the guilt of the defendants.

The tribunal was truly shocked, however, by the wrenching stories of utter inhumanity told by witnesses who actually saw murders being committed or had survived Nazi camps. Their tales spoke of unsurpassed cruelty and brought tears to the eyes of those in the courtroom. Clumsy attempts at cross-examination by the defense only made the witnesses' testimony that much more compelling.

The *Einsatzgruppen*

Hitler's SS was indicted at Nuremberg as a criminal organization. SS crimes included not only its operation of the Nazi concentration and death camps, but also the murders committed by the notorious *Einsatzgruppen*, or action groups. Originally organized in 1939–1940 to exterminate Polish priests, doctors, lawyers, teachers, writers, and other intellectuals, the *Einsatzgruppen* soon expanded their operations. Following the German invasion of Russia in 1941, the *Einsatzgruppen* continued to kill intellectuals and political opponents, but their primary focus shifted to the annihilation of Jews. The SS divided their *Einsatzgruppen* into four geographically organized groups that followed behind the advancing German armies. When they encountered Jews, they murdered them in large- and small-scale shooting operations. An estimated 1.3 million Jews fell victim to *Einsatzgruppen* bullets during the early years of the Second World War.

Otto Ohlendorf (standing at microphone), commander of a special SS unit assigned to kill Jews in southern Russia, testified that all the defendants knew of the murders he and his men committed.

The Prosecution's Final Blow

Jackson and the other prosecutors maintained the momentum generated by the witnesses. The French team offered hard evidence concerning the hideous medical experiments performed on inmates at Nazi camps. The British pressed Dönitz and Raeder on the issue of abandoning helpless British sailors at sea; the Americans did likewise when it came to the murders of Allied aircrews shot down over Germany. The Russian prosecutors showed the court ghastly slides of executions and mutilated dead bodies. Looking at these pictures, Göring horrified everyone in attendance, including his lawyer and some of his codefendants, by smirking, chuckling, and at one point pretending to read a book.

Exhausted but satisfied, the prosecution finally turned the courtroom over to the

The Ship *Laconia*

The case against the German admirals, in particular Karl Dönitz, went beyond the Commando Order. It extended to a related command, issued in 1942 by Dönitz himself, in which the admiral told his submarine captains in the Atlantic not to pick up survivors from torpedoed ships. The order came down after German U-boats were attacked by British aircraft while attempting to rescue sailors and others from the sinking British ship *Laconia*. Standard practice in naval warfare dictated that after a ship sank, the vessel responsible for its sinking was supposed to make every reasonable effort to rescue people in the water. In the *Laconia*'s case, German submarines pulled British sailors and Italian POWs, who were being transported to a prison camp by the ship, from the sea, put them into lifeboats, and headed toward shore. Even though the Germans sent out a radio message in English announcing their peaceful intent, British airplanes attacked the U-boats as they floated on the surface. Dönitz responded with his order to leave survivors to their own devices—and was subsequently charged with committing a crime on the high seas.

Admiral Karl Dönitz was accused of committing a crime on the high seas because he ordered German submarine commanders not to rescue survivors from torpedoed ships.

defense attorneys. The tribunal ordered the German lawyers to open their case on March 7. For over two months Jackson had worked to convict the defendants. Now the Germans had the almost impossible task of trying to find some way out from under the weight of the evidence against their clients. They needed to convince the tribunal that even if the defendants were not completely innocent, they were not guilty of the specific charges against them. It would not be an easy task.

Chapter Five

Nazis on the Stand

By the first week of March 1946, after almost three months, the prosecution had completed its presentation to the tribunal. Jackson's prosecutors had left most people in the courtroom convinced of the twenty-one defendants' guilt. The defense now had the job of undermining what appeared to be an airtight case. The defense lawyers knew it would be impossible to argue against their clients' general guilt, since the evidence had already proven that, so they decided to refocus the tribunal's attention on the details of the specific charges. The lawyers could not exonerate the men on trial, but they could try to persuade the judges that their crimes had been of a lesser degree. The men were guilty, in other words, but not as charged.

The Defense Opens: Göring

Göring's defense began first, under extremely tight security. The Allies still feared an attempt to disrupt the trial by rogue SS men who remained at large. Before the end of the war the Nazis had set up a secret terrorist group known as Werewolf. The members of this organization, who were supposed to function as insurgents, had been given the mission of attacking Allied targets after Germany had surrendered. No known operations of any significance had taken place since the immediate postwar period, but the Werewolf threat continued to loom. The tribunal grew especially cautious concerning Göring after an incident in the fall of 1945. While Göring was being escorted to the courtroom one day, an SS dagger mysteriously plummeted from somewhere above and landed at his feet. The authorities responded by ordering the construction of a covered walkway connecting the prison and courtroom. Now that Göring's defense was about to begin, security was tightened even further, including the assignment of extra guards inside and outside of the Palace of Justice.

The Göring Defense

Hermann Göring had a lawyer, but when it came time to counter the charges against him, Hitler's former number-two man spoke for himself. Göring answered the charge of conspiracy by noting that he functioned as part of what was at the time a legitimate government, not a criminal gang. If by conspiracy the prosecution meant one intended to kill the Jews, Göring said that was sheer nonsense. He told the court that a conspiracy required advance planning, and the murder of Jews was not planned in advance. Therefore, there could not have been a conspiracy at all. As for crimes against humanity, Göring held that only Hitler and Himmler had the authority to order Germans to kill millions of people. He himself had neither the power nor the desire to see the Jews dead. Göring told the tribunal that he sought only to have the Jews excluded from German social and political life; he never wanted them killed. In terms of Count Two, making aggressive war, Göring claimed that every war was essentially aggressive, because every nation had war plans drawn up before fighting actually took place. Therefore, he reasoned, what Germany had done could not be considered a crime.

Unlike Dönitz's smooth and sophisticated defense, Göring's was straightforward, aggressive, and bold. Unfortunately for Göring, his efforts did not yield the results he hoped for.

Hermann Göring testifies in his own defense in September 1946.

The mystery dagger missed its mark, but the prosecution's evidence did not. Jackson's team had shown clearly that Göring controlled much of what happened in the Nazi regime. Göring's lawyer tried to counter the prosecution by calling one witness after another who had worked with his client, trying to show that he had been just doing his job as a loyal German official. The tactic failed miserably. The prosecution, led by Maxwell-Fyfe, systematically dismantled each witness's story.

Next, Göring himself took the stand, determined to do a better job in his own defense than had his lawyer. Cool, confident, and eager to do battle with the prosecutors during cross-examination, Göring laughed off the conspiracy charge. He said that he was an important man in the Third Reich; his codefendants were bit players. "One can only talk of conspiracy," he said, "to the extent that this took place between the Führer and me."[54] The rest of the men on trial, Göring continued, had been too low in the Nazi hierarchy to be included in any master plan. Still, he vehemently denied any responsibility for persecution and mass murder.

Jackson, sensing that Göring might gain the upper hand, decided to cross-examine the defendant himself. Mustering all of his verbal skill, Jackson repeatedly tried to crack Göring on the stand. Göring, however, finally getting the fight he wanted, countered every move the American made. Göring's command was so apparent that the British judge Birkett noted in his diary,

> Göring is the man who really dominated the proceedings . . . nobody appears to have been prepared for his immense ability and knowledge, and his thorough mastery and understanding of the details of captured documents. The cross-examination had not proceeded more than ten minutes before it was seen that he was the complete master of Mr. Justice Jackson. Suave, shrewd, adroit, capable, resourceful, [Göring] quickly saw the elements of the situation,

and as his confidence grew, his mastery became more apparent.[55]

When Jackson tried to introduce statements made by Göring that had been secretly taped in his cell, Göring challenged their admissibility. He had apparently been promised that his conversations would not be taped. Suddenly, Jackson found himself on the defensive.

Jackson's frustration grew and soon became evident to everyone in the courtroom. At one point Jackson lost his temper and complained to the judges of what he considered to be Göring's "arrogant and contemptuous attitude toward the Tribunal which is giving him the trial he never gave a living soul, nor dead one either."[56] Göring chuckled as the judges simply told Jackson to continue with his cross-examination. Maxwell-Fyfe and Rudenko proved no more successful against the clever Göring; he swiftly outwitted and outmaneuvered them as well. Rudenko, perhaps the most aggressive of the prosecutors at Nuremberg, confronted Göring directly with the crimes of the Nazi regime. Despite Rudenko's careful descriptions of what Hitler's people had done, Göring held firm.

When Göring finally stepped down, Jackson and his battered prosecutors breathed a sigh of relief and prepared for the rest of the defendants. *Life* magazine summed up Göring's testimony by telling its readers that the ex-Nazi had done on the stand precisely what he set out to do. "Arrogant, crafty, intelligent," the magazine wrote, "Göring obviously enjoyed himself as he kept the courtroom spellbound for days. . . . Göring was anxious, whatever his fate, that history record him as an important world figure and as a German hero."[57]

Moving On: Hess

Rudolf Hess was supposed to follow Göring, but his lawyer feared that Hess's confused mental state might hurt his case more than help it. Throughout the trial Hess had been distracting the court with his odd behavior. He might at any given moment be seen staring at a book without turning a single page, smiling to himself, or simply looking at the ceiling with a blank expression on his face. When confronted, Hess fell back on his primary defense—his supposed amnesia. Pushed on any point, Hess would simply say that he had no recollection of the event.

Hess's attorney worried most of all about what might happen if his client suddenly decided to discuss before the tribunal his two favorite subjects—space aliens and the Jewish plot to hypnotize everyone in Germany, including himself. Consequently, Hess never testified in his own defense, even though he told the court that he had sufficiently recovered his memory. His lawyer, in fact, only called two witnesses, neither of whom gave any significant evidence of Hess's innocence. The rest of Hess's case was built on documents that were somewhat unrelated to the charges against him. It seemed impossible to defend a man with such deep psychological problems. Taylor, the American prosecutor, wondered "whether Hess . . . would have been more appropriately confined in a mental institution than a jail."[58]

Still, many people in the courtroom wondered just how disabled Hess really was. At times it seemed that he was play-acting at being ill rather than suffering from any genuine disorder. Hess's alleged disabilities, for instance, did not prevent him from commenting to Göring that someday all of the defendants would have to pay for their crimes. Hess was obviously convinced of his own guilt, even though he repeatedly claimed not to understand the accusations made by the prosecution. Gilbert, the prison psychologist, often caught glimpses of a Rudolf Hess who knew very well what was going on. On one occasion Gilbert asked Hess up front, "How do we know you are not simulating your loss of memory?"[59] Hess replied weakly that he had no reason to lie. He apparently overlooked the fact that he was on trial for his life, which provided a very good reason indeed.

More Denials

Göring and Hess set the tone for the pleas of ignorance and convenient amnesia that came from the men who followed them on the stand. Von Ribbentrop claimed that he was just a diplomat; he knew nothing of crimes against humanity. Keitel and Jodl both portrayed themselves as simple soldiers who knew nothing of any crimes and were simply doing their duty. Kaltenbrunner not only denied involvement in the Final Solution, which his security office oversaw, he actually claimed to have opposed it. Even when presented with documents carrying his signature and ordering murders, the former SD chief denied everything. Asked repeatedly

Hermann Göring (left) and Karl Dönitz (center) discuss the trial as Rudolf Hess (right) looks on.

about his role in the extermination of the Jews, Kaltenbrunner gave the same answer—he had nothing to do with it. Not only the tribunal but also the other defendants found that hard to believe.

Similar responses came from Rosenberg and Streicher. Rosenberg had been advised by Göring to simply say he served Hitler but had nothing to do with any killings. Thus, during an especially heated cross-examination by American prosecutor Dodd, he held to the ignorance defense. Dodd pressured Rosenberg about his duties as the minister for the Eastern territories. The prosecutor demanded to

know from the defendant whether or not Jews had been murdered in areas of Russia under Rosenberg's direct control. Rosenberg tried to evade the question, but Dodd eventually forced him to give a reply. Dodd asked bluntly for a yes or no reply. Trapped and exhausted, Rosenberg admitted to having knowledge of the killing of Jews.

The British prosecutor who had responsibility for cross-examining Streicher thought he would have an easier time than the lawyer who questioned Rosenberg. Streicher had publicly supported the Nazi terror in the pages of his newspaper, *Der*

Stürmer. The prosecutor was thrown off guard, however, when the former publisher claimed to have no knowledge of the very murders he encouraged and justified in the columns he wrote. Streicher told the tribunal that he did not know that Jews would be the target of the Final Solution, despite the fact that he wrote in a 1939 article that the "Jews in Russia must be killed. They must be utterly exterminated."[60] With the paper in front of him, Streicher still held to his assertion that he had no role in the genocide.

Cracking on the Stand

The defense attorneys brought their clients to the stand and tried their best to put distance between them and the crimes of

Julius Streicher denied all knowledge of the murder of Jews, despite having advocated the killing of Russian Jews as early as 1939.

Hitler and the Nazis. The prosecutors, however, proved to be even more effective at cross-examination than in the presentation of their own cases. Using heaps of incriminating evidence at their disposal, Jackson and his men furiously countered the defendants' attempts to argue ignorance. In some instances the ferocity of the prosecution's attacks prompted a total collapse of the men who stood before the court.

On the stand, Funk was challenged by the same Dodd who had forced Rosenberg to admit his knowledge of the genocide in Russia. Dodd lost no time in focusing the judges' attention on Funk's role in taking gold stolen from dead Jews and turning it into cash that the SS could use to pay for its bloody work. According to the trial transcripts, as presented in Telford Taylor's book *The Anatomy of the Nuremberg Trials: A Personal Memoir*, Dodd came straight to the point with Funk:

"When did you start to do business with the SS, Herr Funk?" Dodd began.

"Business with the SS? I have never done that," Funk replied.

"Yes sir, business with the SS. Are you sure about that? . . . I ask you again, when did you start to do business with the SS?"

"I never started business with the SS?"

"Just a minute. Were you in the habit of having gold teeth deposited in the Reichsbank?" Dodd continued.

"No," Funk answered once again.

"But you did have [gold] from the SS. Did you not?"

Seemingly hiding something, Funk merely said, "I don't know."[61]

Dodd wanted to make sure that he gave Funk every opportunity to deny what everyone in the court already knew: Funk, as head of the Reichsbank, had taken gold from the Jewish victims of the Nazi terror and used it to finance Hitler's criminal regime.

Dodd gave Funk one more chance to admit his guilt. Dimming the lights, the audience in the courtroom saw a film of gold fillings and other dental work ripped from the mouths of Jews killed at the death camps in Poland. Many in the room turned away; others stared in shock and disgust. The Nazis robbed the dead to pay their bills, and Funk's bank had been at the center of it. While the movie continued to roll, Dodd drew close to Funk, and noted for the tribunal that the gold they saw on the screen was melted down and deposited in the bank that Funk operated. Funk might never have seen the gold except as bars brought to his bank's door, but that was not the point. "The trouble was there was blood on that gold," Dodd said turning to look into Funk's face, "was there not, and you knew this since 1942."[62] As the American prosecutor walked back to his seat, Funk swallowed hard, blinked quickly—and began to cry.

Funk's unspoken yet dramatic admission of guilt was surpassed only by the emotion-packed testimony of Frank. Faced with irrefutable evidence of his complicity in the murder of millions of Jews while he was the Nazi governor of Poland, Frank confessed openly in court before the entire world. The spectacle began when his own defense attorney asked Frank a question that triggered perhaps the most famous outburst of remorse and regret from any former Nazi. Hoping for a vague response, Frank's lawyer asked, "Did you ever participate in the annihilation of Jews?" Frank broke down and declared, "I say yes . . . my conscience does not allow me to throw responsibility solely on [others] . . . if Adolf Hitler has laid that dreadful responsibility on his people, then it is mine too. . . . A thousand years will pass and still this guilt of Germany will not have been erased!"[63] The tribunal finally heard one of the men who made the Nazi terror possible own up to the blame that had been placed upon him. The prosecution told the judges that it had no further questions for the defendant.

Admissions, False and Genuine

Speer was, in Taylor's words, "the last of the 'big' defendants—those few who had . . . risen to the top of the Nazi hierarchy."[64] Unlike the others, however, he went out of his way to take responsibility on the stand for the role he played in Hitler's plan. He presented a picture of himself as a conscientious bureaucrat who worked to curb the excesses of his colleague and codefendant Sauckel. Sauckel had been the mastermind of the Nazi forced labor program, Speer claimed. The mistreatment that took place was over his objections. Speer also argued that far from being a diehard Hitler supporter, he actually evolved into an anti-Nazi by 1945. Speer reminded the tribunal that he had plotted to kill Hitler near the end of the war, because he finally accepted the fact that his hero had betrayed him.

Speer admitted some guilt, but he never did so without reservation. He claimed that he was to blame for being part of a government that had tormented Europe, yet Speer was reluctant to hold himself personally responsible for what he had done as one of Hitler's closest aides. In his prison cell Speer acted every bit the remorseful ex-Nazi in his conversations with Major Leon Goldensohn, the prison psychiatrist. To Goldensohn, Speer acknowledged that history would prove that the trials were necessary because the defendants needed to be punished. Everyone knew, Speer said, that "Hitler's government was criminal," and he was "made party to the use of forced labor, although Sauckel is the one who supplied it."[65] Some of the judges and prosecutors thought Speer's admission of guilt to be genuine. His codefendants, on the other hand, felt that he was simply trying to avoid being hanged for his part in the terror.

Speer likely was angling to keep his head out of a noose, but the remorse expressed by von Schirach and Fritsche was undeniably real. Fritsche lamented the fact that he had willingly followed a criminal leader and had placed his communication skills at the disposal of murderers.

Walther Funk headed the Reichsbank, where gold stolen from Jewish victims was deposited.

He even rather unfairly took on the burden for the extermination program directed at the Jews: "On the basis of my work, 5 million people were murdered and untold atrocities took place."[66]

Von Schirach, for his part, admitted that he had passed on Nazi lies to young people and twisted their minds in Hitler's service. The former Hitler Youth chief con-fessed that he had led German boys and girls into the depths of crime and disgrace. He swore to the tribunal, "Before God, before the German nation, before my German people, I alone bear the guilt of having trained our young people . . . for a man who murdered millions [in] the most devilish mass murder known to history. . . . It is a crime which fills every German with

The Speer Defense

Albert Speer certainly had the most complex defense among those offered at Nuremberg. Speer organized his around a three-part strategy. First, he held himself up as a restraining influence on the Nazi labor organizers. Next, Speer exaggerated his determination to assassinate Hitler in 1945. Finally, as a last resort, he admitted his guilt and expressed the deepest remorse publicly before the tribunal.

Speer gave the court details of his supposed effort to improve the lives of slave laborers and forced workers. He even claimed to have actually saved a number of lives. Thanks to him, Speer said, many fewer unfortunate men and women fell into the clutches of the real villain, labor chief Fritz Sauckel. Speer also outlined his alleged plan to kill Hitler using, of all things, Zyklon B pellets. Speer told the judges that he finally realized his error in supporting Hitler's regime, and he became convinced that only by murdering his führer could he end the war and save Germany.

When these arguments fell short, Speer accepted blame for his part in the Nazi government. He admitted that Hitler's regime had been a criminal one and that his own greatest mistake was in serving it and believing Hitler's lies. This final ploy proved convincing enough to save Speer from the hangman's noose.

Albert Speer claimed to have secretly opposed Hitler, and even to have plotted to assassinate the Nazi leader.

shame."[67] Von Schirach was sincere in his recognition that he had poisoned the minds of a generation of children. Along with Fritsche, von Schirach did what few of the defendants were willing to do—accept responsibility not only for their actions but also for the long-term consequences of those actions.

The Organizations

The individual defendants had testified and had been cross-examined. Some were contrite; others were defiant. After the last of them sat down, the defense turned its efforts toward the organizations indicted by the tribunal. Eight attorneys had the responsibility for mounting a defense of the Nazi organizations, and they had only one month to do it. They had to act quickly, and they did. The defense team offered as evidence tens of thousands of signed affidavits from former SS men alone and compiled a list of six hundred potential witnesses who could bolster their case. Disappointingly for the defense, only twenty-two actually took the stand. All this was in an effort to convince the court that groups such as the SS, Gestapo, and military high command did nothing more than follow orders in Hitler's service. The real criminals, in other words, were the men who gave the orders— Himmler and Hitler.

Still, nothing seemed to persuade the judges. The Nazi organizations on trial were implicated in the worst crimes, and all of the evidence seemed to prove their guilt. The SS, in particular, could not evade responsibility for the shooting and gassing of Jews. The SS had been Hitler's chosen weapon in his program to kill every Jew in Europe. Its members had been caught on film, in photographs, and in documents trying to do just that. The SS was not alone, though. American prosecutor Dodd pointed out that all of the indicted organizations, including the high command and the Nazi Party leadership, bore equal shares of the guilt. "The fact is," Dodd told the court, "that all of these organizations united in carrying out the criminal program of Nazi Germany. They are to blame."[68]

After months of attempting to defend the indefensible, the attorneys for the accused men and organizations on trial at Nuremberg rested their cases. The German lawyers had worked to prove that while their clients might have been Nazis, they were not guilty of the charges contained in the tribunal's indictments. Now, the defense and the prosecution turned their attention to composing their closing arguments as the participants prepared for the trials' last act.

Chapter Six

Judgment

The Nuremberg trials now moved into their final phase. The court's emphasis shifted from discovery and examination to the decision on the guilt or innocence of the twenty-one defendants. The proceedings to this point had been exhausting and, at times, frustrating. Both teams of lawyers had struggled to prove their cases. The prosecution urged the tribunal to convict all of the ex-Nazis and exact from them the heaviest price possible. The defense pleaded with the judges to consider the unique circumstances that had faced the defendants and to be lenient in the interest of healing old wounds. The defense and prosecution alike recognized this part of the trials as being, in essence, the real end of World War II in Europe. As the judges prepared to hear the closing arguments of each team, they reflected on their responsibility to see that justice be done in the fairest manner possible. Even though many voices around the world called out for vengeance, Lawrence and his colleagues knew that they had to punish, but they had to do so in the purest spirit of the law.

The Defense Speaks

The International Military Tribunal gave the defense counsels fourteen days at the end of August 1945 to sum up their arguments. Although they had been working together up until then, at this point each of the defendants' lawyers determined his own strategy. Some of them tried to convince the court that their clients were actually just little men who inflated their Nazi stature. Rosenberg, Funk, and Streicher were all portrayed by their lawyers as essentially powerless men who liked everyone to think that they were more important than they really were. Streicher's attorney, for example, dismissed his own client as a lunatic and braggart to whom no one ever listened. He was guilty of spitting out hateful but ultimately empty words, so it was claimed.

Other defense lawyers tried to emphasize their clients' good sides. The generals and admirals, in particular, were cast as honest military men who were too loyal to perceive the consequences of their actions. Raeder was offered up as a proud career navy man whose only crime was not thinking about the orders he followed. Raeder's attorney, in fact, argued that the admiral was a good Christian who had done nothing wrong. "Raeder cannot be a criminal," his lawyer told the court, "since all his life he has lived honorably and as a Christian. A man who believes in God does not commit crimes, and a soldier who believes in God is not a war criminal."[69]

Speer's lawyer claimed that his man was an anti-Nazi who deserved the court's appreciation rather than condemnation. The former armaments minister, so his attorney contended, had worked to counter the worst aspects of Sauckel's labor policies; indeed, Speer had actually saved many lives. The judges were told to take

One of the defense lawyers addresses the court during the Nuremberg Trials.

into consideration not only Speer's efforts to improve workers' conditions but also his plan to assassinate Hitler in early 1945. Speer had served Hitler, but he was certainly not guilty of the charges against him, his lawyer said.

The lawyer representing Schacht made perhaps the most persuasive closing argument. He held that his client could not possibly be a criminal, because Schacht himself had been a Nazi victim. In 1944 Schacht had been sent to a concentration camp for supposedly plotting against Hitler. His attorney now suggested that a guilty verdict would make no sense. He pointed out that he once "was assigned to defend Schacht before Hitler's People's Court; in the summer of 1945, I was asked to conduct his defense before the International Military Tribunal."[70] Schacht could not be, his lawyer concluded, simultaneously both a perpetrator and a victim.

The Prosecution Takes Its Turn

Despite great effort, the closing arguments made by the defense came across weakly. Nobody in the courtroom, least of all the judges, was moved by the vague assertions of innocence offered by the lawyers for the ex-Nazis. The charges were too serious and the evidence too convincing. There was very little that could be held up to prove that the men in the dock had not, at one time or another, helped Hitler implement his plans for world domination and genocide.

Jackson stressed this point as he presented the prosecution's closing argument. Precise and methodical, Jackson implicat-ed each defendant in turn as he summed up what the prosecution had contended since the trial began. Göring, Jackson said, was "the man who tied the activities of all the defendants together in a common effort . . . he stuck his pudgy fingers in every pie."[71] Hitler's former second in command thus bore a special and burdensome share of the guilt.

Keitel, Jodl, Raeder, and Dönitz had betrayed their military honor and given the German armed forces over to a madman who used them to wage war on Europe. Kaltenbrunner, Jackson continued, had the blood of millions on his hands. Funk, he claimed, had been blinded by stolen gold. Jackson argued that Sauckel and Speer had served Hitler as little more than global slave drivers. Schacht, Fritsche, von Papen, and von Neurath were guilty of willful, calculated ignorance. The prosecution held that these men hid for twelve years from the reality of the Nazi regime in order to further their own careers.

In a final crushing blow to the defendants' cases, Jackson ended his presentation by accusing each man at Nuremberg of being Hitler's accomplice in a bloody crime spree that brought misery to an entire continent. The men in the dock nurtured the power that Hitler used to torment, enslave, and kill millions of people. Hitler's guilt then, Jackson said, "is the guilt of the whole dock, and every man in it."[72]

Final Statements

On August 31, 1946, the trial aspect of the proceedings ended. The judges then offered each of the twenty-one defendants

In his closing argument, prosecutor Robert H. Jackson (at podium) stressed that all the defendants in one way or another had helped Hitler perpetrate his crimes.

fifteen minutes for any final comments they might want entered in the trial record. The tone and substance of the readings that followed varied greatly from man to man. Seyss-Inquart, Streicher, and Göring were all unrepentant. They told the court that they stood by their actions and had nothing to apologize for. They said that they had served Hitler loyally; each promised that he would do it again if given the chance. Sauckel and the commanders acknowledged no guilt for specific crimes, but they did express a remorse that eluded Göring and his comrades. Sauckel, in particular, seemed genuinely sorry for his part in the Nazi program. In front of the

judges, Sauckel claimed to regret ever having done anything to help Hitler: "I have been shaken to the depths of my soul by the atrocities revealed in this trial. . . . My error was perhaps the excess of my feelings and my confidence in, as well as my great veneration of Hitler. The Hitler of this trial I could not recognize. . . . I myself am prepared to meet any fate which providence has in store for me."[73] Keitel and Jodl expressed similar sentiments. They had sacrificed their honor and dignity for an evil cause. They, like Sauckel, were ready to accept their punishment.

Rudolf Hess finally threw off the camouflage of amnesia. Confronted with the distinct possibility of a guilty verdict and a possible death sentence, Hess at last seemed to recall his Nazi past. He still believed that Jews threatened him and the world, and he wanted the court to know that what he had done in Hitler's service would one day be considered heroic. "I was permitted," Hess told the tribunal, "to work for many years of my life under the greatest son whom my people has brought forth in its thousand-year history. Even if I could, I would not want to erase this peri-od of time from my existence." Hess con-cluded by saying that "I am happy to know that I have done my duty to my peo-ple, as a German, as a National Socialist, as a loyal follower of my Führer. I do not regret anything."[74]

One after another the defendants read their final statements to the court. When they had finished, the tribunal calmly moved to adjourn. The judges, after view-ing evidence and listening to witnesses for almost a year, called the proceedings to a

close. "The tribunal," Lawrence declared, "will now adjourn until 23 September. . . . On that date the judgment will be announced."[75]

The Judges Deliberate

The discussions that followed were serious, thorough, and often heated. On several key points the tribunal members disagreed with one another, most often when it came to the degree of guilt to be assigned to men such as Schacht and Fritsche. The Russians considered both men to be as guilty as the rest, but the American and British judges felt strongly that Schacht and Fritsche functioned outside of the Nazi decision-making machinery. Rudolf Hess's fate was also a point of contention. The tribunal agreed that he was guilty; the only question was whether or not he deserved to die for his crimes. The Russians, once again, wanted the defendant to pay the ultimate price, but the other judges were reluctant to sentence Hess to death.

The decision on Göring was a foregone conclusion; here there was unanimity on the bench. Göring was guilty on all counts and should be hanged. Likewise the judges were in complete agreement on Rosenberg, Frick, Frank, Keitel, Jodl, Kaltenbrunner, and Seyss-Inquart. They would all hang. Streicher was included in this group, even though he had not been part of the Nazi government. He had helped drum up support not just for the war effort but, worse still, for the Nazi extermination program. Judge Parker's aide, Major Robert Stewart, wrote that Streicher was "a cheerleader [who] never carries the ball nor calls a play, yet by his continual goading of the crowd to frenzied excitement he is a personality in his team's success."[76]

The disputes and disagreements among the tribunal members forced the court to extend its deliberations to September 30, 1946. The judges needed more time to

Hans Frank (standing) makes a statement during the Nuremberg Trials.

consider subtle legal details in the cases of Speer, Dönitz, von Papen, and several other men. Judgment day was thus postponed for the defendants sitting anxiously in Nuremberg's prison. In their cells, the accused passed the time as best they could. Some of the men played cards, others wrote letters or statements explaining their actions for future generations to read. Schacht, Raeder, Göring, and von Ribbentrop visited with their families after many months of separation. Schacht, in particular, took solace in the words of his four-year-old daughter, who barely knew her own father. Whispering through the visiting room's wire screen that stood between them, the little girl told Schacht, "I like you very much."[77] Fritsche drew comfort and confidence from a discovery he made on one of his daily walks. Strolling through the prison yard, he found a four-leaf clover lying on the ground.

The Verdicts Come In

On Monday, September 30, the waiting ended. After the usual wake-up call in the cell blocks, the defendants were led to the courtroom under very tight security. The men entered and assumed their places in the dock as the technicians switched on radio microphones. The entire proceeding that day would be broadcast live over German radio. As the radio equipment hummed and lights were turned on, the judges slowly filed in and took their seats.

At exactly 9:30 A.M., Lawrence spoke. In the case of Göring, he began, "The record discloses no excuses for the man."[78] Lawrence pronounced him guilty. He also announced guilty verdicts for Hess, von Ribbentrop, Keitel, Jodl, and von Neurath, all of whom played key roles in the Nazi regime's efforts to enslave Europe. Taking turns, the judges then issued guilty verdicts against Rosenberg, Frank, and Seyss-Inquart. When Lawrence announced the guilty verdict in Streicher's case, he said that Streicher's incitement "at the time when the Jews in the East were being killed"[79] represented a clear case of assisting in mass murder. Dönitz, Frick, Speer, and Sauckel were similarly found guilty of crimes against the world.

Fearing the worst, Schacht, Fritsche, and von Papen sat silently. In Schacht's case, the tribunal declared, there was no evidence of participation in the Nazi conspiracy. He had helped organize Nazi finances, but had not aided their crimes—not guilty. Fritsche and von Papen, the judges similarly contended, should have resisted Hitler's pull more forcefully, but neither man had an active role in implementing the Nazi policies that led to war and murder. The men were found not guilty as charged.

In total, eighteen convictions and three acquittals were pronounced, and then the court recessed until the afternoon. Schacht, von Papen, and Fritsche burst into smiles, lit cigars, and celebrated by devouring the pieces of fruit left on their lunch plates by Andrus, their former jailor. As for the rest of the men, they sat quietly and picked at a meager meal as convicted criminals.

Sentencing

The court resumed its work at 2:30 in the afternoon. One by one the guilty men were led before the judges. Göring, as always,

"Death by Hanging!"

Just before von Ribbentrop became the first convicted Nazi criminal to die, the commandant of the Nuremberg prison made his rounds. Andrus walked through the cellblock where the condemned men were housed, stopping by each cell to repeat the tribunal's sentence. At each heavy metal door, Andrus called out the prisoner's name and, as quoted in Robert Conot's book *Justice at Nuremberg*, said in a flat voice, "Death by hanging!"

Hanging was the traditional form of punishment for criminals denied a more honorable death, such as being shot by a firing squad. The hangman at Nuremberg was Sergeant John C. Wood, a veteran of 375 military executions by hanging. He was in charge of every detail of his assignment at Nuremberg. Wood ordered specially made hemp rope for the executions, oversaw the construction of the gallows, and even tied each noose himself.

The hanging process was identical for all of the men condemned by the court. The prisoner was taken from his cell at the appointed time and led to the gallows alone. Once there, he was escorted up the scaffold's thirteen steps to the execution platform. Next, he was asked for any last words, and then he had a black hood placed over his head. The rope was draped around his neck and the knot tightened. The noose was arranged so as to break the man's neck as he fell. Finally, a lever was pulled, and the prisoner dropped to his death. Doctors stood by, ready to certify that the man was indeed dead. After that, the body was cut down, photographed, and sent for disposal.

American army sergeant John C. Wood, inspects a noose like the ones used in the execution of those condemned for Nazi atrocities.

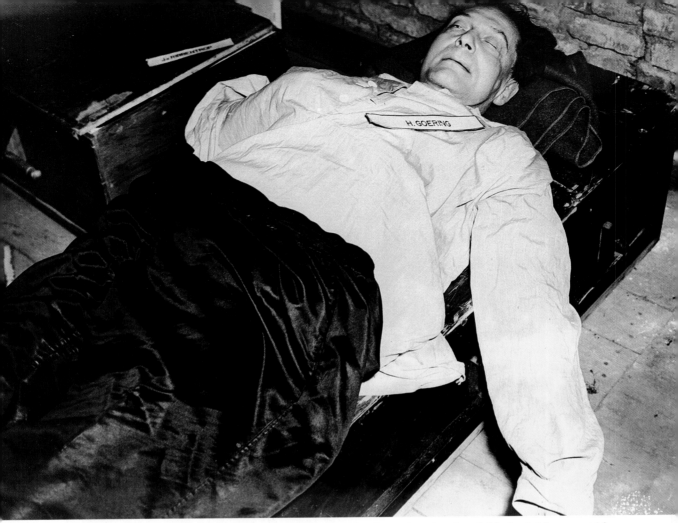

Hours before he was scheduled to hang, Hermann Göring committed suicide by taking cyanide that he had kept hidden since before his capture.

went first. Speaking for the court, Lawrence addressed the former Nazi leader in a matter-of-fact tone: "Defendant Göring, on the count of the indictment on which you have been convicted, the International Military Tribunal sentences you to death by hanging."[80] Göring repeated the word "death" softly as he was returned to his prison cell. Hess stood gently swaying back and forth, staring at the ceiling of

the courtroom, as the court sentenced him to life in prison. Hitler's former deputy had no response.

The judges handed down sentences to the Nuremberg criminals without dramatics, only a steady drumbeat of ultimate justice. Frank, von Ribbentrop, Keitel, and Jodl were told they would die at the end of a rope, even though Jodl had requested that he be shot like a soldier. Streicher,

Life After Acquittal

Lucky to escape the noose or life in a cold prison cell, Fritsche, Schacht, and von Papen left Nuremberg as free men. Fritsche's liberty did not last long, though. He was detained by a German denazification court in 1947 and was held for three years. These special courts, set up to erase every remnant of Nazi ideas and institutions in Germany, often retried men found not guilty of war crimes by the Allies. Fritsche used his time in jail profitably, however, in writing his memoirs, which were later published. Fritsche was eventually cleared and released in 1950. He lived a quiet life until he died of cancer in 1953.

Schacht was similarly detained by a German court and tried in 1948; unlike Fritsche he was convicted. Facing a long prison sentence, Schacht won a last-minute appeal and was set free. He went on to open his own trade bank, becoming a very wealthy man. Like Fritsche, Schacht decided to tell his story in print and wrote his autobiography in 1953. Schacht died in March 1970.

Hitler's onetime vice-chancellor, von Papen, also was convicted by a denazification court and freed on appeal. The high point of von Papen's post-Nuremberg life came when he, too, published his memoirs. In the book von Papen explained his support for the Nazis in much the same way he did before the International Military Tribunal. Von Papen contended that he recognized Hitler's true nature very early on and, from that point, withdrew his loyalty and support. He lived the rest of his days uneventfully, dying in May 1967 at the age of eighty-nine.

Following their acquittal, Franz von Papen (left), Hjalmar Schacht (center), and Hans Fritsche (right) meet with members of the press.

The Last Lonely Prisoner

Of the Nuremberg defendants sentenced to life in prison, only Hess served his full term. Hess and the others were transferred to Berlin's Spandau Prison after their sentencing in 1946. There, Hess watched forlornly as his fellow inmates either did their time and left or, in the case of life terms, won early release. For the last twenty-one years of his life, from 1966 to 1987, Hess remained alone in Spandau. The releases of Speer and Schirach made him the facility's only resident. Hess spent his final empty years watching his guard detachments change monthly between the four Allied powers. He wandered the prison grounds, gardened, and relaxed in the makeshift gazebo built just for him by his jailors. All the while, Hess waited for word of his own release; it never came. Despite pleas for clemency by the United States and Great Britain, both of which felt further imprisonment would serve no useful purpose, the Russians refused to let Hess go. They were determined that the last living Nazi should symbolically pay the price for the crimes of the regime he served.

Left with no hope, Hess took matters into his own hands. In August 1987 he walked into his gazebo, tied an electrical cord to the window frame, and hanged himself. Rudolf Hess was ninety-three years old. Following his death, Spandau Prison was demolished, and the rubble, like the wreckage of Nazi Germany itself, was cleared away to make room for a new Berlin and a new nation.

Seyss-Inquart, Kaltenbrunner, Frick, Rosenberg, and Sauckel all heard the dreaded phrase "death by hanging" spoken after their names. Speer received twenty years in prison, as did Von Schirach. Von Neurath was given fifteen, Dönitz ten years. Raeder and Funk were sentenced to spend the rest of their lives behind bars.

By 3:40 P.M. the greatest trial in history had ended, and justice had been done to the largest extent possible at the time. Immediately, the prisoners condemned to die were separated from the others. The men who received prison sentences went back to their cells before being transferred to the facility where they would serve their time. The men who would hang went to their cells to endure the fifteen-day wait for execution.

The Final Moments

The prisoners spent their last days contemplating the end of their lives. Families were allowed to visit once again, to say goodbye. Lawyers assisted some of the condemned in writing last-minute appeals. Priests and ministers were made available to those, like Frank, who wanted to ask for God's forgiveness.

The days passed slowly. On the night before the executions, all was quiet until a guard cried out, "Göring's having a fit!"[81] The cell block suddenly erupted with activity. The silent prison echoed with calls of alarm as soldiers and doctors rushed to Göring's cell. They arrived too late; the first men in the room found the prisoner dead on the floor. Pretending to use the toilet, Göring had removed a poison capsule from its hiding place inside a tobacco pipe. He had put it between his teeth and bitten down before anyone knew what he was up to. Hermann Göring, the second most powerful man in Hitler's Germany, cheated the hangman by taking his own life.

Göring's suicide prompted the prison authorities to handcuff the remaining prisoners and place a guard in each cell. The soldiers remained on duty throughout the night.

At precisely 1:05 A.M. on the morning of October 16, 1946, von Ribbentrop was taken from his cell to the gallows. He walked calmly to the noose, up the thirteen steps that rose to the hangman's platform. The executioner placed a black hood over von Ribbentrop's head, and then a rope. Ten minutes later the ex–foreign minister, who had implemented a Nazi policy of aggression, dropped to his death. One by one his comrades met the same fate. The generals, the admirals, and the administrators of terror went to the gallows and were hanged. The final member of Hitler's once dreaded government to die, Seyss-Inquart, when asked if he had anything to say, replied, "I hope this will be the last act of the tragedy of the Second World War."[82] He swung dead at the end of a rope at 2:57 A.M.

The bodies of the dead were gathered up and driven out to what had been the Nazi concentration camp at Dachau. The corpses, in a moment of bitter irony, were then cremated in the very ovens designed to erase from history the victims of Adolf Hitler's vicious regime. Without ceremony, the resulting ashes were dumped into a nearby creek and disappeared forever.

Justice After Nuremberg

The executions in the fall of 1946 ended the trials of the major war criminals, but the larger project of bringing former Nazis to justice continued. Thousands of trials and other court proceedings took place in the decades that followed. These ranged from criminal trials of SS men and camp guards to civil lawsuits against German companies that supported the Nazi war effort and annihilation program.

The legal process beyond Nuremberg actually began even as the prosecution of the twenty-one major defendants was still underway. While the prosecution teams pressed Göring and the others at the Palace of Justice, the British were pushing forward with other cases. From September to November 1945 the British put the staff of the Bergen-Belsen concentration camp on trial. Four months later, in March 1946, British lawyers opened their case against the manufacturers of Zyklon B, the poison used to murder a million Jews at Auschwitz.

After the international proceedings at Nuremberg, the Americans held their own follow-up trials. American tribunals, between December 1946 and April 1949, heard cases against former army and SS officers, ex-Nazi doctors, German industrialists, and the lawyers, judges, and government officials who operated the machinery of Hitler's regime on a daily basis. Called the Subsequent Nuremberg Trials, these efforts to widen the scope of the postwar prosecutions resulted in further convictions being handed down to guilty Germans and their accomplices.

Similarly, the French and Russians continued to try to convict former Nazis and Nazi collaborators guilty of crimes against the world. French courts convicted thousands of such people, sentencing nearly two thousand of them to death. By 1950 the Russians had put more than thirteen thousand men and women behind bars for their roles in bringing the Nazi terror to Russia.

The New Germans Take Over

The process of meting out justice changed, some would say slowed, after 1950, when the Allies transferred most of their legal authority to the newly established German courts. Established separately in the parts of Germany occupied by the Western Allies and the Russians, these new West and East German courts had an inconsistent record in terms of convictions. Even though proceedings were initiated against over one hundred thousand people, only around ten thousand were tried and convicted in West Germany and perhaps a further twelve thousand in East Germany. The low number of convictions was followed by sentences considered by some historians to be absurdly lenient. The historian John Weiss, in fact, has written that the German "courts . . . slapped on the wrist those who had slaughtered Jews"[83] and others.

Many of the German trials after 1950 could indeed be labeled failures. The trials of ten SS men in 1958, for example, turned out to be a mockery of justice. The men were duly convicted of killing hundreds of Jews, but they were sentenced to a mere two days in prison for each of the murders they had committed. Between 1963 and 1965 twenty-one men who had

Although war crime trials continued into the sixties, German courts were inconsistent in obtaining convictions.

Lt. Col. Seichi Ohta (left, with his translator) was one of seven Japanese war criminals who were sentenced to death by the International Military Tribunal for the Far East.

worked and murdered at Auschwitz came before a West German tribunal. Five of the former SS officers received life sentences, but the rest were each sentenced to only six years behind bars. During the 1950s and 1960s sentences were often lenient, and the men sent to prison were in many instances released early.

The Nuremberg Legacy

Despite the many judicial setbacks that came after the major trials, the Nuremberg legacy is a proud one. That the subsequent trials were held at all was due to the example set by the proceedings against the major criminals in 1945 and 1946. Considering the millions of Germans who had belonged to the Nazi Party, it would have been impossible to try them all. According to one writer, "if the victorious powers had actually tried to convict every Nazi, most Germans would have to be thrown in prison."[84] The very existence of an active judicial process was a matter for celebration; that major Nazi criminals could be sorted out from their colleagues and accomplices and punished represented genuine success.

The truly lasting impact of the Nuremberg trials, however, cannot be measured simply by looking at records of the criminal trials aimed at bringing justice to ex-Nazis. The trials set new precedents and established a new global intolerance for persecution and mass murder. Indeed, after the Japanese surrender in World War II in September 1945, a special tribunal along the Nuremberg lines was established for the Far East. Even as the proceedings in Germany were getting under way, judges were sitting down in Tokyo to administer justice in the cases of twenty-eight Japanese leaders accused of committing atrocities in Asia. Using the standards developed for the Nuremberg trials, the International Military Tribunal for the Far East heard testimony for 417 days, eventually convicting twenty-five Japanese defendants. Seven of these men were sentenced to death; life in prison awaited the rest. No one would be able to ignore terror and genocide again without thinking about the courtroom at Nuremberg, its spirit, and the example that it set.

By placing international criminal figures in the dock and trying them before the world community, Nuremberg also served as a model for future international courts of justice. In addition, the people judged in those courts would no longer be able to claim ignorance or duty as excuses for their offenses. Not knowing or simply obeying the orders of superiors could not be used to argue for one's innocence in the face of hideous crimes against humanity. The people held responsible for oppression and mass murder in places as far apart as Cambodia, Rwanda, and Bosnia had no recourse to the so-called Nuremberg defense because the judges at Nuremberg took it away from them and other international criminals. Men and women called before judges to answer for what they have done can no longer use the excuses offered by Göring, Hess, Frank, and the rest. This one set of trials, then, left an enduring mark on history by focusing the world's attention on instances of inhumanity and holding people, especially leaders, responsible for their actions. The Nuremberg trials impacted the future by doing justice fairly, when justice needed to be done.

Notes

Introduction: The Crime and the Criminals

1. Quoted in Michael Burleigh, *The Third Reich: A New History.* New York: Macmillan, 2000, p. 383.
2. Quoted in James M. Glass, *"Life Unworthy of Life": Racial Phobia and Mass Murder in Hitler's Germany.* New York: Basic Books, 1997, p. 83.

Chapter 1: Taking Prisoners

3. Quoted in Richard Overy, *Interrogations: The Nazi Elite in Allied Hands, 1945.* New York: Penguin, 2001, p. 6.
4. Quoted in Overy, *Interrogations,* p. 8.
5. Quoted in Joachim Fest, *The Face of the Third Reich: Portraits of the Nazi Leadership.* New York: De Capo, 1999, p. 75.
6. Quoted in Fest, *Face of the Third Reich,* p. 72.
7. Quoted in Robert E. Conot, *Justice at Nuremberg.* New York: Carroll and Graf, 1983, p. 32.
8. Quoted in Gitta Sereny, *Albert Speer: His Battle with the Truth.* New York: Alfred A. Knopf, 1993, p. 355.
9. Quoted in Eugene Davidson, *The Trial of the Germans: An Account of the Twenty-two Defendants Before the International Military Tribunal at Nuremberg.* Columbia: University of Missouri Press, 1966, p. 438.
10. Quoted in Davidson, *Trial of the Germans,* p. 335.
11. Quoted in Davidson, *Trial of the Germans,* p. 349.
12. Quoted in Conot, *Justice at Nuremberg,* p. 32.
13. Quoted in Conot, *Justice at Nuremberg,* p. 72.

Chapter 2: Interrogations

14. Quoted in G.M. Gilbert, *Nuremberg Diary.* New York: De Capo, 1995, p. 100.
15. Quoted in Overy, *Interrogations,* p. 63.
16. Quoted in Overy, *Interrogations,* p. 88.
17. Quoted in Overy, *Interrogations,* pp. 148–49.
18. Quoted in Davidson, *Trial of the Germans,* p. 38.
19. John K. Lattimer, *Hitler and the Nazi Leaders: A Unique Insight into Evil.* New York: Hippocrene, 2001, p. 89.
20. Quoted in Overy, *Interrogations,* p. 145.
21. Quoted in Davidson, *Trial of the Germans,* p. 61.
22. Quoted in Overy, *Interrogations,* p. 285.
23. Overy, *Interrogations,* p. 121.
24. Quoted in Overy, *Interrogations,* p. 503.
25. Quoted in Conot, *Justice at Nuremberg,* p. 79.
26. Quoted in Overy, *Interrogations,* pp. 167–68.

Chapter 3: Prosecutors, Defenders, and Judges

27. Quoted in Conot, *Justice at Nuremberg*, p. 59.
28. Quoted in Conot, *Justice at Nuremberg*, p. 19.
29. Quoted in Davidson, *Trial of the Germans*, p. 553.
30. Quoted in Davidson, *Trial of the Germans*, p. 553.
31. Quoted in Michael R. Marrus, *The Nuremberg War Crimes Trial, 1945–1946: A Documentary History*. New York: Bedford/St. Martin's, 1997, p. 65.
32. Quoted in Marrus, *Nuremberg War Crimes Trial*, p. 70.
33. Quoted in Gilbert, *Nuremberg Diary*, pp. 5, 7.
34. Telford Taylor, *The Anatomy of the Nuremberg Trials: A Personal Memoir*. New York: Alfred A. Knopf, 1992, p. 133.
35. Quoted in Conot, *Justice at Nuremberg*, p. 83.
36. Quoted in Conot, *Justice at Nuremberg*, p. 83.
37. Conot, *Justice at Nuremberg*, p. 69.
38. Quoted in Conot, *Justice at Nuremberg*, p. 63.
39. Quoted in Conot, *Justice at Nuremberg*, p. 18.
40. Quoted in Conot, *Justice at Nuremberg*, pp. 20–21.

Chapter 4: The Prosecution Opens

41. Quoted in Gilbert, *Nuremberg Diary*, p. 36.
42. Quoted in Marrus, *Nuremberg War Crimes Trial*, p. 78.
43. Quoted in Marrus, *Nuremberg War Crimes Trial*, pp. 79–80.
44. Quoted in Marrus, *Nuremberg War Crimes Trial*, p. 83.
45. Quoted in Marrus, *Nuremberg War Crimes Trial*, p. 79.
46. Quoted in Conot, *Justice at Nuremberg*, p. 146.
47. Quoted in Gilbert, *Nuremberg Diary*, p. 45.
48. Quoted in Gilbert, *Nuremberg Diary*, p. 49.
49. Quoted in Marrus, *Nuremberg War Crimes Trial*, p. 87.
50. Quoted in Conot, *Justice at Nuremberg*, p. 199.
51. Quoted in Conot, *Justice at Nuremberg*, p. 200.
52. Quoted in Conot, *Justice at Nuremberg*, p. 233.
53. Quoted in Conot, *Justice at Nuremberg*, p. 281.

Chapter 5: Nazis on the Stand

54. Quoted in Conot, *Justice at Nuremberg*, pp. 333–34.
55. Quoted in Conot, *Justice at Nuremberg*, p. 338.
56. Quoted in Davidson, *Trial of the Germans*, p. 88.
57. Quoted in Conot, *Justice at Nuremberg*, p. 346.
58. Quoted in Taylor, *Anatomy of the Nuremberg Trials*, p. 350.
59. Quoted in Gilbert, *Nuremberg Diary*, p. 217.
60. Quoted in Conot, *Justice at Nuremberg*, p. 387.
61. Quoted in Taylor, *Anatomy of the Nuremberg Trials*, pp. 394–95.
62. Quoted in Conot, *Justice at Nuremberg*, p. 406.
63. Quoted in Conot, *Justice at Nuremberg*, p. 380.
64. Quoted in Taylor, *Anatomy of the Nuremberg Trials*, p. 448.

65. Quoted in Leon Goldensohn, *The Nuremberg Interviews: An American Psychologist's Conversations with the Defendants and Witnesses.* New York: Alfred A. Knopf, 2004, p. 251.
66. Quoted in Goldensohn, *Nuremberg Interviews*, p. 53.
67. Quoted in Conot, *Justice at Nuremberg*, p. 424.
68. Quoted in Conot, *Justice at Nuremberg*, p. 464.

Chapter 6: Judgment
69. Quoted in Conot, *Justice at Nuremberg*, p. 467.
70. Quoted in Conot, *Justice at Nuremberg*, p. 468.
71. Quoted in Conot, *Justice at Nuremberg*. p. 469.
72. Quoted in Conot, *Justice at Nuremberg*, p. 471.
73. Quoted in Conot, *Justice at Nuremberg*, p. 475.
74. Quoted in Marrus, *Nuremberg War Crimes Trials*, p. 223.
75. Quoted in Conot, *Justice at Nuremberg*, p. 478.

76. Quoted in Conot, *Justice at Nuremberg*, p. 487.
77. Quoted in Conot, *Justice at Nuremberg*, p. 482.
78. Quoted in Gilbert, *Nuremberg Diary*, p. 437.
79. Quoted in Gilbert, *Nuremberg Diary*, p. 443.
80. Quoted in Conot, *Justice at Nuremberg*, pp. 497–98.
81. Quoted in Conot, *Justice at Nuremberg*, p. 504.
82. Quoted in Conot, *Justice at Nuremberg*, p. 506.

Epilogue: Justice After Nuremberg
83. John Weiss, *Ideology of Death: Why the Holocaust Happened in Germany.* Chicago: John R. Dee, 1996, p. 383.
84. Klaus P. Fischer, *The History of an Obsession: German Judeophobia and the Holocaust.* New York: Continuum, 1998, pp. 406–407.

For Further Reading

Books

Linda Jacobs Altman, *Crimes and Criminals of the Holocaust*. Berkeley Heights, NJ: Enslow, 2004. Altman's book is a comprehensive study of the criminal activities of the Nazi regime, with a particular focus on the the final years of the war. The Nuremberg and other trials are dealt with in detail.

Wilbourn Benton, *Nuremberg: The German View of the War Trials*. Dallas, TX: Southern Methodist University Press, 1955. This is a critical look at how the Nuremberg trials were understood by Germans. Along with William Bosch's book, it gives a clear picture of how culture shapes the different ways in which crime and punishment are defined.

William J. Bosch, *Judgment on Nuremberg: American Attitudes Toward the Major German War Crimes Trials*. Chapel Hill: University of North Carolina Press, 1970. This is a thorough study of the myriad ways in which American leaders and the public alike viewed the Nuremberg trials. Of special note here is Bosch's consideration of the impact of the principles established at Nuremberg on the behavior of soldiers in later conflicts, such as the Vietnam War.

Robert H. Jackson, *The Case Against the Nazi War Criminals*. New York: Alfred A. Knopf, 1946. Written by the chief American prosecutor, this book contains documents that Robert H. Jackson considered to be the most important trial materials. Foremost among these is Jackson's own opening statement before the International Military Tribunal, which is offered here in complete text. Jackson's words to the tribunal constitute the clearest explanation to date of exactly what kind of criminal activity the Nazis had engaged in and would be punished for.

Isobel V. Morin, *Days of Judgment: The World War II War Crimes Trials*. Brookfield, CT: Millbrook, 1995. Morin's book helps to put the Nuremberg trials into the larger context of post–World War II efforts to bring war criminals to justice, not just in Germany but in Japan as well. Although the author does not feel that the trials at Nuremberg and Tokyo were a complete success, they did leave a vital historical record of the myriad crimes committed in Europe and Asia during the war.

Earle Rice, *Nazi War Criminals*. San Diego: Lucent, 1997. Rice gives his readers a fine series of portraits of the men behind the crimes being judged at Nuremberg. Most of the major offenders are examined here.

Ann and John Tusa, *The Nuremberg Trials*. Lanham, MD: Cooper Square Press, 2003. This is a single-volume study of the trials that provides a solid overview of the event. The book is well researched and offers a first-rate narrative.

Web Sites

The Avalon Project at Yale Law School: The Nuremberg Trials (www.yale.edu/ lawweb/avalon/imt/imt.htm). The Avalon Project offers access to a complete set of documents relevant to the Nuremberg trials. The text of the indictments, transcripts of testimony, and even trial motions made by the attorneys are included.

The Nizkor Project: The Trial of German Major War Criminals (www.nizkor.org/ hweb/imt/tgmwc). This site gives access to nearly every statement and recorded document associated with the trials. Organized in volumes by date, the material at the site includes verbatim transcripts of courtroom testimony.

The Nuremberg Trials (www.law.umkc. edu/faculty/projects/ftrials/nurem berg/nuremberg.htm). A wealth of information is available here beyond the documentary record. Although pertinent documents are available, the site also contains drawings, photographs of people and places having to do with the trials, and even a cartoon.

Works Consulted

Books

Michael Burleigh, *The Third Reich: A New History.* New York: Macmillan, 2000. This is a fine general history of the Nazi Years which discusses how Hitler came to power and how his regime functioned. Ample space is given to discussion of Nazi crimes of the kind dealt with at Nuremberg.

Robert E. Conot, *Justice at Nuremberg.* New York: Carroll and Graf, 1983. Conot's book is perhaps the best single-volume history of the Nuremberg trials. It covers every aspect of the proceedings from initial capture to the executions. Conot follows the trial almost on a day-to-day basis and provides very good descriptions of the people involved, Nazi and Allied alike.

Eugene Davidson, *The Trial of the Germans: An Account of the Twenty-two Defendants Before the International Military Tribunal at Nuremberg.* Columbia: University of Missouri Press, 1966. Davidson explores the Nuremberg trials in a thematic fashion. After a general discussion of the trial background, the author looks at the cases according to the men and organizations involved. The military, the diplomats, the labor and youth leaderships, among others, are given separate and extensive treatment.

Klaus P. Fischer, *The History of an Obsession: German Judeophobia and the Holo-caust.* New York: Continuum, 1998. This book offers an intriguing overview of the history of Jew-hatred in Germany and how that history drove Germans, including those later charged at Nuremberg, to commit the heinous crimes they did.

G.M. Gilbert, *Nuremberg Diary.* New York: De Capo, 1995. G.M. Gilbert, an American officer and the prison psychologist, gained unique insight into the mental and emotional processes at work within the minds of the men on trial at Nuremberg. His diary reveals much about the criminals and also follows the court proceedings, showing how each man reacted to the experience of having his offenses judged before the world community.

James M. Glass, *"Life Unworthy of Life": Racial Phobia and Mass Murder in Hitler Germany.* New York: Basic Books, 1997. *Life Unworthy of Life* gives a detailed account of the Nazi efforts to kill people they considered to be biologically defective or inferior. Glass shows how a twisted form of scientific certainty helped the Nazis justify their murderous program.

Ian Kershaw, *Hitler: 1936–1945 Nemesis.* New York: W.W. Norton and Company, 2000. *Hitler* is the second volume of a two-volume biography of the Nazi leader. In this volume, Kershaw follows

Hitler through World War II up to the point of his suicide and Germany's defeat.

John K. Lattimer, *Hitler and the Nazi Leaders: A Unique Insight into Evil*. New York: Hippocrene, 2001. A thorough study of the many psychological, physical, and medical problems that plagued the Nuremberg defendants, Lattimer's book is very useful. The author, a staff doctor at Nuremberg, also includes valuable material on such matters as prison operations and the executions of those men condemned to die.

Robert Jay Lifton, *The Nazi Doctors: Medical Killing and the Psychology of Genocide*. New York: Basic Books, 1986. Lifton, in this book, tells the story of the Nazi doctors who selected people to die in the death camps, either through medical experimentation or direct gassing. The author attempts to show how ordinary, perfectly normal physicians could bring themselves to be a part of a murder program that went against everything they stood for.

Michael R. Marrus, *The Nuremberg War Crimes Trial, 1945–1946: A Documentary History*. New York: Bedford/St. Martin's, 1997. This book contains the most significant documents associated with the entire Nuremberg process. From the earliest attempts to organize an unprecedented series of war crimes trials to the post-trial assessments made by political leaders, Marrus's work provides a primary source record of courtroom proceedings and the actual thoughts and words of the trial participants—prosecutors, defenders, and the accused.

Florence R. Miale and Michael Selzer, *The Nuremberg Mind: The Psychology of the Nazi Leaders*. New York: Quadrangle/New York Times Book Company, 1975. Miale and Selzer present the results of the Rorschach tests administered to the men at Nuremberg. The actual test records are given, as are the commentaries offered by the testers.

Richard Overy, *Interrogations: The Nazi Elite in Allied Hands, 1945*. New York: Penguin, 2001. Overy provides a highly detailed account of the interrogations that took place at Ashcan, Dustbin, and the Nuremberg prison. The book contains transcripts of the interrogations, some as part of the story of what Nazi criminals said to their questioners, others as simple documents. *Interrogations* is an excellent book in which to find primary source documents concerning the men at Nuremberg and what they did.

Peter Padfield, *Himmler: A Full-Scale Biography of One of Hitler's Most Ruthless Executioners*. New York: MJF Books, 1990. This book follows the life of SS chief Himmler from his earliest days as an earnest young schoolboy to his suicide in 1945. Himmler is presented as a man obsessed with the goal of creating a pure German race to rule over Europe.

Ralf Georg Reuth, *Goebbels*. New York: Harcourt, 1993. Reuth's biography of Hitler's propaganda chief emphasizes the role of modern technology and communications media in the success of the Nazi program. The author credits Goebbels with convincing the German people to support Hitler's vision.

Gitta Sereny, *Albert Speer: His Battle with the Truth*. New York: Alfred A. Knopf, 1993. Sereny, in this book, offers a glimpse of a man wrestling with his past. Speer is portrayed in the pages of this biography as a career bureaucrat who never fully realized or accepted his role in the tragedy that befell Germany and the world between 1933 and 1945. At times cloaking remembrances in self-pity, Speer never truly comes to terms with his basic guilt.

Telford Taylor, *The Anatomy of the Nuremberg Trials: A Personal Memoir.* New York: Alfred A. Knopf, 1992. Telford Taylor, one of the prominent American figures at the Nuremberg trials, here gives his firsthand account of the proceedings. In the course of his memoir, Taylor gives the reader an opportunity to see with clarity the men and the forces at work at Nuremberg. Full of fascinating detail and insight, Taylor's book is important because it offers the perspective of an eyewitness to Nuremberg.

John Weiss, *Ideology of Death: Why the Holocaust Happened in Germany.* Chicago: John R. Dee, 1996. Weiss discusses the unique features of German history, society, and culture that made it almost inevitable that the Holocaust would begin there. His final chapters cover well the postwar prosecution of Nazi criminals and their accomplices.

Index

Picture Credits

About the Author

John Davenport holds a PhD in history from the University of Connecticut and currently teaches at Corte Madera School in Portola Valley, California. Davenport is the author of several biographies and books on American historical geography. He lives in San Carlos, California, with his wife Jennifer and his sons William and Andrew.